Getting Through to God

Getting Through to God

A book about
communicating
with God —
for yourself,
but mostly
for others

Glenn A. Coon

Review and Herald Publishing Association
Washington, D.C. 20012

Editor: Thomas A. Davis
Book Design: Helcio Deslandes
Cover: Alan Forquer

PRINTED IN U.S.A.

Library of Congress Cataloging in Publication Data

Coon, Glenn A
   Getting through to God.

    1.   Prayer—Study and teaching.   2.   Witness
bearing (Christianity)—Study and teaching.
3.   Evangelistic work—Study and teaching.
I.   Title.
BV214.C66   248.4   80-16899

CONTENTS

PREFACE

The title of this book is truly intriguing. It suggests it is possible to get through to God and that we may be sure we can. It also implies that many of God's people need to learn how to hold more effective communication with the Lord. If, in fact, "prayer is the breath of the soul" *(Messages to Young People,* p. 249), and if "it is a part of God's plan to grant us, in answer to the prayer of faith, that which He would not bestow did we not thus ask" *(The Great Controversy,* p. 525), then we had better learn the joy of victorious prayer.

Perhaps no one in our church has had more experience in dealing with these issues than the writer of this volume. He has conducted "The ABC's of Prayer" and related seminars in all parts of the North American Division, and has traveled extensively in other divisions with his classes and lectures.

The Lord has invited us to ask if we would receive, knock if we would have an opened door, and seek if we would find. It is obvious, then, that though every good impulse is placed in our hearts by the Holy Spirit, the initiative rests with us. Why do we not receive more from God? Because we do not ask as we should. Why are not more doors opened for us? Because we do not knock. Why do we not find more evidences of the divine hand in our lives? Because we do not seek.

On the basis of the fact that the answer to our needs is found in the precious promises of God, the author leads us into basic considerations regarding the purpose and plan of prayer. He calls upon us to exercise more genuine faith in God and to claim more and more of the precious promises contained in His Word. There is not a genuine need in our lives that has not been provided for in God's great treasure house. "Prayer is the key in the hand of faith to unlock heaven's storehouse, where are treasured the boundless resources of Omnipotence."—*Steps to Christ,* pp. 94, 95.

There is no reason why we should be underprivileged, poverty-stricken, helpless children when the Living God is our Father, the Son of God is our divine Saviour, and the richness of the Holy Spirit is made available to us. Let us then experiment with prayer in a true and meaningful way. Let us take God at His word, and know the full joys of His salvation and His providences in our lives.

N. R. Dower

INTRODUCTION

The supreme joy of life is sharing. The supreme joy of the *Christian* life is sharing *Christ.* It is a pleasure to let others know that Christ and we are interested in them, especially when they are loaded with problems. There is joy also in being interested in the continued happiness of those who have found a degree of rest in Jesus.

I have often heard "mature" Christians tell of the duty to share one's faith with others. While it is a duty for the Christian to share his faith, yet the joy of doing so far surpasses the duty. People may misunderstand Christianity if we fail to be joyful when sharing our faith in Jesus.

Humanity Is Social. Our Lord made us social beings. We hunger for human sympathy, fellowship, understanding, and love.

"We love him, because he first loved us" (1 John 4:19). Soul-winning communication is the art of reaching the heart of another with the message of Christ's love. Since it is the love of Christ that wins, this new relation is like a courtship—a sacred, pure, spiritual courtship. This relation to Jesus changes the new believer's attitudes toward other people. He does not belittle others (Phil. 2:3), or complain (verse 14), or speak evil of any person (Titus 3:2).

Begin Small. At Creation, human fellowship began with two persons. Jesus sent His disciples out two and two. He promised that where two or three gather in His name, He Himself will be present. So, let two or three band together for soul winning. But prayer fellowship need not be limited to that number. It could eventually involve the whole church.

Getting Through to Others. Getting through to others is often more easily accomplished by two than one, in harmony with the example of Jesus when He sent out the seventy.

In the lessons in this book we have developed seven secrets for reaching the heart of a troubled soul. We share these in our "Personal Message" section following each study. The lessons will show how and why we often fail to get through to others, and how, under the leading of our Lord, we may use these secrets to find the path to the human heart. By offering to that open heart the promises of our Lord, we make it possible for a new nature to be formed and a new birth consummated (1 Peter 1:23; 2 Peter 1:4).

Begin With a Prayer Partner. We recommend that you try to find another Christian who will meet with you once a week for one hour, unless you have already expanded your fellowship into a prayer circle.

Format of Weekly Prayer Fellowship Hour. It is important to keep the prayer hour informal and casual. Here is a list of suggestions to help you proceed.

1. You may choose to have an opening chorus.

2. One or more may then offer an opening prayer. We recommend that you use a definite Bible promise each time you pray together. Open the Bible to a promise such as Luke 11:13 and place your hand on the promise as a gesture of simple trust. Then pray a

three-part prayer during the first part of the Prayer Fellowship Hour. This prayer will be explained in Lesson 2. Later, you will also learn how the three-part prayer can be condensed into a single-sentence prayer. The prayer is based on the ABC's of prayer, which are

A Asking, Matt. 7:7.

B Believing, Mark 11:24.

C Claiming, or receiving, Matt. 21:22.

You may wish to pray in unison, reading the following three-part prayer:

"Dear Lord, we *ask* You for the presence of the Holy Spirit as promised in Luke 11:13. We *believe* You are hearing us and guiding our thinking. We *claim* the answer to our prayer and we thank You, in Jesus' name, that we are now experiencing His presence. Amen."

3. Each person in the Fellowship should have a Study Guide. Each one, by turn, may read a paragraph aloud and then make a brief comment concerning the concept it contains. Thus reading and commenting on one paragraph after another, the Study Guide is followed for about thirty minutes. We suggest that the reading of the Study Guide, and the comments on it, be limited to thirty minutes, even if the Guide is not completed during the Prayer Fellowship Hour.

4. Ten or fifteen minutes may then be spent in sharing with one another the answers to prayer that have resulted from claiming specific Bible promises. (We suggest that during the Prayer Fellowship Hour only those answers to prayer received by claiming specific Bible promises be shared.)

5. Those in the Fellowship will select one person each to visit before the next Fellowship Hour. It may be one who has become discouraged, has illness in the family, or for some other reason needs Christian encouragement through a personal visit.

6. Prayer is offered by all present for each one selected to be visited. The promise for a soul who is

spiritually discouraged may be 1 John 5:16 or Hebrews 2:14, 15. A promise for one out of work may be Matthew 6:33 or Philippians 4:19. A promise for parents whose children are losing their way might be Isaiah 49:25. With the Bible open before them, those present may offer a three-part prayer such as:

"Dear Lord, we ask You to save John Doe [Jane Doe] according to 1 John 5:16. [The text might be read beforehand.] We believe you are in the process of seeking to do this as we follow the methods of our Lord in getting through to him [her] and we thank You in Jesus' name that we are actually receiving the answer promised. Amen."

Note: The following quotation may greatly encourage your hearts as you think of the sinner's power to choose wrongly and, on the other hand, the power of God in answer to prayer in taking hold of the sinner's deep-down desire *not to be lost.* "Let the workers grasp the promises of God, saying, 'Thou hast promised, "Ask, and ye shall receive." I must have this soul converted to Jesus Christ.' "—*Medical Ministry,* p. 244.

7. The prayer listed under suggestion 6 may also be the benediction. You may choose to sing a chorus before the prayer is offered.

Outside the Fellowship Hour the lips of all members are to be sealed concerning the problems of people for whom the group is praying. Furthermore, the group should not discuss the individual's problem when it is brought up only to be prayed about. The problem is merely identified briefly and then prayed about. The person having the problem should be visited with during the week before the Fellowship Hour.

8. Before you visit the person you have selected, practice what you have learned from the Study Guide material. By studying these special personal messages carefully, you will learn how to approach others who have heavy burdens, as we all have had.

9. We should be very humble in visiting with any person (Phil. 2:3). This is important. We should never have a holier-than-thou attitude. Never joke about such matters as the individual's not having attended church. Tenderness, and an interest in every one of his legitimate needs, is a key to getting through to him. Then, when he sees we are humble and loving, when he sees we are concerned about and praying for his needs for a job, or recovery from illness, for example, we may tell him of our weekly Fellowship Hour and perhaps invite him to meet with us.

Should he come to the Fellowship Hour, he adds someone in whom he is interested to the list of persons being prayed for and visited. In this way he is made a part of the group and never feels belittled or like an outsider.

10 If this individual has not been attending your church, he will quite likely eventually want to go with you. Later, he may wish to ask questions concerning problems. You will then be able to either share scriptural answers with him or introduce the pastor or some church worker to him to aid him in his quest for scriptural light.

At no time is there to be any pressure exerted. There is plenty of time for doctrinal studies. What the soul needs is fellowship in Christ.

1

OH, GOD, DO YOU CARE?
Our Wonderful Problem Solver

"If ye then, being evil, know how to give good gifts unto your children: how much more shall your heavenly Father give the Holy Spirit to them that ask him?" (Luke 11:13).

Many years ago, during the dead of winter, the 18-month-old daughter of a Boston, Massachusetts, minister became ill with a fever. While she was sick, a raging blizzard arose and lasted for several days. Coincidentally, with the abating of the storm the little girl's fever abated also. She had not eaten for several days, but now, with the sinking of the fever, her weakened body called for nourishment, and her appetite began to return.

Dragging herself out of bed, she walked unsteadily over to where her mother sat. Looking up into Mother's eyes, she spoke one word: "Apple." Mother knew there was not an apple in the house. She turned and looked in the direction of her husband. The little girl followed Mother's eyes and started in Daddy's direction. Placing both hands on her father's knee, she looked pitifully up into his face and said, "Apple?"

The father looked into the pale, pinched face of his little girl for a moment. He thought of the long distance between his home and the place where he might get an apple. Then he arose and began to put on his outdoor clothes.

Plunging into the deep whiteness, he struggled to

where he thought he might get that which would fulfill the desire of his little daughter's heart. On and on he went. Finally he secured an apple, fought his way back to his home, and placed the prize in his little one's shaking hand.

Why did he go through all this exhausting effort to get one apple? Parents know it was because he was a daddy, and he loved his little girl.

God, your heavenly Father, is more eager to respond to your legitimate requests than that loving father was to satisfy the pleading of his tiny daughter. Won't you pause right now, look up into the heavens, and thank Him as your prayer-answering Father?

Multitudes of professed Christians approach God, but most of them do so with a wrong attitude. They think they must overcome His reluctance. They have an insufficient grasp of His loving character. They have never yet seen God as one who is eager to answer prayer. Their words testify to this misunderstanding. Their countenances often reflect this negativism. The words they use in prayer express a doubt of His willingness to do what He has promised.

It is the purpose of this lesson to change such attitudes. We are horrified at the story of the jungle woman throwing her baby into the mouth of a crocodile, thus hoping to overcome her god's reluctance to answer her prayers. Yet, many professed Christians seem to see God as just about as unwilling to answer their prayers. So few see the true God, the loving God, as He really is. We want to see Him that way in this lesson.

Jesus stated the great truth that "he that hath seen me hath seen the Father" (John 14:9). We must study truth in the light of our Lord's character. Doctrine takes on its meaning when we study it in relation to Jesus Christ, His attitudes, and the character of our great heavenly Father, whom Jesus reveals. Note the following eight points about God:

1. God Is Looking for Someone to Aid. "And other sheep I have, which are not of this fold: them also I must bring, and they shall hear my voice; and there shall be one fold, and one shepherd" (John 10:16).

2. Look to Calvary and Capture the True Picture of God. "He that spared not his own Son, but delivered him up for us all, how shall he not with him also freely give us all things?" (Rom. 8:32).

Let us illustrate this text by an imagined situation.

It is a beautiful Sunday afternoon, and we are picnicking with Pastor and Mrs. Brown and their son, Jim. Our son, Jack, is with us. He and Jim plunge into the swift-flowing river as we parents chat casually together on the bank.

A large oak tree supplies the shade on this warm day. The river, in time of flood, has washed away the soil from under part of the root system of the tree. The long, large roots with their many rootlets still protrude into the river, creating a possible hazard to those who dive. One might dive between the large roots, only to be caught fast. And, alas, this happens to our Jack.

Now, Jim is a lifeguard. He is an expert at lifesaving. He dives under the surface and manages to extricate our unconscious Jack from the clutches of those roots.

But, under the water, without oxygen, and with fighting the surging waters, Jim is weakening. He is able, however, to lift Jack up to us. With almost superhuman effort he manages to get Jack to where we can grasp a hand and drag him out of the water. But we can't catch Jim. He slips back into the water and goes under. While we are resuscitating Jack, Jim's parents try frantically to reach him. But the swift-flowing river carries him far downstream. His lifeless body is finally discovered, caught by some bushes. Jim died to save my son, Jack.

A sad funeral service takes place three days later. Jack and we stand with tear-stained cheeks beside Pastor and Mrs. Brown as we look upon Jim's still form. He is in his casket with flowers all around. But flowers and tears cannot bring Jim back.

Jack turns to Pastor Brown and says, "I can never, never forget what Jim did for me." He cannot restrain the tears of sympathy and appreciation. There's a big tear on Pastor Brown's cheek as he answers, "Jack, you cannot know how deep is our sorrow that Jim is gone. We are happy he could save you. We are glad that only one of you died. And Jack, you know how much we love you."

With deep emotion Jack replies in one word, "Absolutely!"

At the graveside, our son and we stand again next to Pastor and Mrs. Brown. "Jim's brave act will never be forgotten by me," our son says solemnly but emotionally. And he adds, "Your willingness to let him risk—and lose—his life for me is almost beyond comprehension."

As the committal service ends, my son once again, in inexpressible emotion, speaks to Pastor Brown, "I will never forget, as long as life shall last, your attitude in all this."

A few weeks later my wife and I are called out of town suddenly. We leave Jack in charge of our house. He reads and works about the place. He prepares some important papers for his next day's classes. In his concentrated study he eats little all day. In the evening he wonders whether there is any mail in the mailbox outside. So he slips through the door and, forgetting to take the key, locks himself out of the house.

He tries every door and all the windows he can reach. Alas, every one is locked. His keys, his billfold, and his change purse are all inside. He suddenly realizes his weariness and his hunger. Night is coming, and he is outside his house. "How foolish I was!" Jack exclaims in self-reproach.

He tries the doors again, then the windows. All is in vain. Must he sleep outdoors without even a jacket to protect himself from the frost?

Then he remembers that Pastor and Mrs. Brown live just a few blocks away. A happy thought brings him relief. He will go to the Browns' home for the night.

But on his way doubt fills his mind. Will the Browns accept him?

When Pastor Brown answers the doorbell Jack bursts into tears. He blurts something like, "Pastor Brown, I am in trouble." Pastor Brown tries to speak a word of comfort, but in vain.

"Pastor Brown," Jack starts again, "I am in great trouble. But I do not know whether you would be willing to help me."

Pastor Brown looks on in amazement. Our son continues, "I have been thinking of you, and have wondered whether you really love me."

Before Pastor Brown can get a word in edgewise, our son continues, "Pastor Brown, I have locked myself out of my own home, but I feel that I am imposing on you. I need help, but I am not sure you are interested in me."

Pastor Brown can scarcely believe his ears. Jack is in trouble, but he is also in great doubt. He actually doubts the willingness of the pastor to help him.

Finally the pastor is able to speak. "Jack," he begins tenderly and reprovingly, "have you already forgotten the river?"

"Oh, forgive me," Jack replies shamefacedly. "It completely slipped my mind."

When my wife and I return the next day, we are chagrined to hear what happened. "Jack, why did you question Pastor Brown's willingness to give you a place to sleep? Why did you for a single moment doubt that he would gladly give you a nice warm supper?"

Our son replies sheepishly, "Dad, I forgot the river."

Need we draw a parallel? When we doubt our heavenly Father's willingness to come to our aid, have we forgotten a hill called Calvary?

3. Think of God as Often Giving Us Something Better Than We Ask. "I will bring the blind by a way that they knew not; I will lead them in paths that they have not known. . . . These things will I do unto them, and not forsake them" (Isaiah 42:16).

We often tell an experience we had with our daughter, Juanita, which took place when she was only a tiny tot. I walked into our front room one day to see her placing a razor blade in her mouth. God gave me quickness of thought. I smiled, hoping she would imitate me. She did, and never closed her mouth on the blade. I walked slowly toward her, smiling continually. I quietly repeated the words, "Nita, Nita." This kept her attention so she never closed her mouth but continued to smile broadly. With my thumb and index finger I reached into her mouth, still wide with a smile, picked out the razor blade, and set her free. Then I spoke commandingly, "Juanita, that blade would have cut up your mouth."

We then supplied her need for food, but not by giving her what she thought was food—razor blades. We knew the better way. God always answers the prayer of sincere faith. But he reserves the right to answer that prayer the very *best* way—the way we would wish, could we fully understand all the circumstances.

A friend of ours relates an interesting experience he had with a beggar on the street. This man asked our friend for a quarter, to which he replied, "No." As the beggar was turning to speak to the next person my friend called to him, "Sir, I am not going to give you a quarter. I am going to give you a dollar." And he did just that.

Picture that beggar returning home. He tells his family that a man said No to his request for a quarter. Had the beggar stopped there, he would have been guilty of two things: (1) misstating the facts; (2) misrepresenting my friend.

So for us to picture God as saying, "No, period!" is misrepresenting Him. God never says to His believing child, "No, period." He may sometimes say, "No, comma," meaning, "You are not asking for one quarter as much as I want to give you!"

4. Think of God as Truthful. "God is not a man, that he should lie; neither the son of man, that he should repent: hath he said, and shall he not do it? or hath he spoken, and shall he not make it good?" (Num. 23:19).

A minister who read the Old Testament through sixty-nine times and the New Testament seventy-one times says he discovered at least 3,573 promises in the Bible. Others claim to have found more, as many as seven or eight thousand promises.

A woman approached a minister, saying she had a problem about forgiveness. The minister pointed her to the promise of 1 John 1:9: "If we confess our sins, he is faithful and just to forgive us our sins, and to cleanse us from all unrighteousness."

The minister pointed out that the condition to this promise is that she confess her sins. She explained to the minister that she *had* confessed her sins—hundreds of times, for forty years. He then suggested that they kneel down and claim the promise, which they did. The minister arose with strong assurance on his face that the woman was completely forgiven. But her response was still one of grave doubts. The minister said, assuringly, "You are now forgiven, aren't you?"

"That is what I'm afraid to say," she replied, her countenance clouded with doubt. The minister asked her whether she believed the Bible. Her reply was a positive Yes. He asked her whether she believed the Bible promises. The answer again was a firm Yes. Then he asked her whether she believed the particular promise of 1 John 1:9. She still gave a firm Yes. The minister, just to be sure, asked her once more whether she had confessed all her sins. She replied she had confessed all she was aware of. The Holy Spirit then seemed to impress him to ask a searching question: "If the Holy Spirit should point out one sin you have not confessed, would you be willing to confess that also?"

The woman unhesitatingly replied with a fervent "Yes, I surely would!"

"What about the sin brought to view in 1 John 5:10 in the middle of the verse?" the minister asked. "It says, 'He that believeth not God hath made him a liar.' What about confessing that sin you have committed for forty years?"

The minister spoke so kindly and his face registered such Christlike tenderness that the reproof went like a dart straight to her heart. She saw that she had been committing a very great sin in not believing God. She had been making God a liar.

"Let us get down on our knees!" she exclaimed. And there she confessed her sin of making God a liar for so many years. Then she asked the minister to claim God's promise for her. She sobbed out her joyful confidence that she was now forgiven. As they arose to their feet she exclaimed, "Just think of it, pastor, I could have had complete forgiveness and cleansing forty years ago had I but believed God."

It is "impossible for God to lie" (Heb. 6:18).

5. Think of God as Powerful Enough to Bring Solu-

tions. "By the word of the Lord were the heavens made; and all the host of them by the breath of his mouth. . . . For he spake, and it was" (Ps. 33:6, 9). "Through faith we understand that the worlds were framed by the word of God" (Heb. 11:3).

When the authors of these lessons were grasping the true dimensions of prayer, two texts of Scripture came alive in a flood of illumination. They are (1) Romans 4:17, "God . . . calleth those things which be not as though they were"; and (2) Psalm 33:9, "He spake, and it was." Together the two passages of Scripture say, in effect, that anything that *does not* exist, *does* exist the moment God speaks it. This is God's creative power.

6. *Have Childlike Faith.* "Except ye be converted, and become as little children, ye shall not enter into the kingdom of heaven" (Matt. 18:3).

Children are humble and believing.

How does childlike faith express itself? Remember the story of the little girls discussing a point on which they disagreed? When one said, "It is so," the other replied, "It tain't so."

The first girl, in order to give weight to her statement, replied, "Yes, it is so, because Mother said it is so."

But the other little girl did not *know* her friend's mother, so she spoke with a shrug of the shoulder, "It still tain't so."

This stirred the first girl to reply with great earnestness and conviction, "It is so, too, because what Mother says is so, is so even if it tain't so." This is childlike faith.

7. *Visualize the Solution.* Jesus taught us to offer a prayer that *asks, believes,* and then actually *receives,* or *claims,* the solution without doubting, because what God says is so, even though our own limited intellect cannot comprehend it all.

Jesus commands us to:

ASK—Matthew 7:7, "Ask, and it shall be given you."

BELIEVE—Mark 11:24, "Believe that ye receive . . . and ye shall have."

RECEIVE, or CLAIM—Matthew 21:22, "All things, whatsoever ye shall ask in prayer, believing, ye shall receive." (Here we use the words *receive* and *claim* interchangeably. When we go to the airport baggage claim, for instance, we *claim* our baggage in order to *receive* it.)

8. *Claim God's Creative Promises.* "Whereby are given unto us exceeding great and precious promises: that by these ye might be partakers of the divine nature, having escaped the corruption that is in the world through lust" (2 Peter 1:4). "Create in me a clean heart, O God; and renew a right spirit within me" (Ps. 51:10). "Now ye are clean through the word which I have spoken unto you" (John 15:3).

Study Guide 1

A Personal Message

One of the first decisions of a born-again Christian is to share his faith in Jesus with others. In many cases the one who starts this sharing program is almost shocked. He learns that there is a barrier between him and the one for whose salvation he is burdened.

Christ's mission to this world 2,000 years ago is the same as His mission through each converted soul. He wants the soul winner and the individual won to be able eventually to say as Paul said of Jew and Gentile, "He . . . hath broken down the middle wall of partition between us" (Eph. 2:14).

To help you who use these Study Guides let the Christ in you break down the barriers between you and loved ones and others for whom you are burdened, we present in this section, two vital secrets for reaching hearts.

The first secret is Christ's humility. When we visit one who has not been in church for some time, that person needs to see us "clothed with humility" (1 Peter 5:5).

This humility will manifest itself by not condemning him for being absent from church. It will not suggest how foolish he was to have left the "truth" by saying, "You know the truth." Humility will not try to bring conviction to the one we are seeking to help. This is the work of the Holy Spirit (John 16:8).

Humility will not merely cause us to say we have

missed the absentee—it will go farther. (We could say all these things and still appear to have a holier-than-thou attitude.) If we have missed the absentee, we must tell him *why* in such a way that he will not feel we are preaching to him or belittling him. Humility will say a word to him that will indicate honor and deep respect for him (Phil. 2:3; 1 Peter 2:17). We may tell him we miss him; his being away makes us lonesome because he is a part of us. There is a certain emptiness at the house of worship when he is not there.

There are many ways of letting him know we miss him without giving him any thought that we are of the opinion that we are better than he.

Another factor in getting through to him, in breaking down barriers, is to "confess your faults" (James 5:16). We may say, "Brother, I have come to apologize for any unkindness or coldness we have shown you, and I am asking you to forgive all of us." If we know of some *specific* thing we ourselves have done, we will confess this. Humility, however, will not suggest to him that *he* was in any way guilty of the misunderstanding, even though he may have been twenty times as guilty as some of us.

Jesus made clear the results of being clothed with humility: "he that humbleth himself shall be exalted" (Luke 18:14).

While our apology to the absent member does not refer to *his* part in the wrong, we will not "side" with him against the other Christians in the church.

Quiz

1. We should think of God as a very good .... (Luke 11:13).
2. In John 10:16 Jesus shows that God is like a .... looking for ....
3. Romans 8:32 tells us that God .... gives us all things.
4. God brings us by a way we know .... (Isa. 42:16).
5. Our Lord wants to give us abundantly above all we can ask or .... (Eph. 3:20).
6. The worlds were framed by the .... of God (Heb. 11:3).
7. God requires us to become like .... (Matt. 18:3).

Correct Answers

1. Father
2. shepherd, His sheep
3. freely
4. not
5. think
6. word
7. little children

Assignment

We recommend that you review this lesson. In this way you will receive much more benefit than from a single reading. Try drilling yourselves on the principles taught. The second, third, or even fourth review will give you more comprehension of the Study Guide than a single reading.

We suggest that in the Fellowship Hour you discuss the lesson. Each one present may talk about what was particularly helpful to him. By repetition the mind holds the truths presented. Also, study carefully at home the section in each Study Guide. Come prepared to discuss various ways by which you think you could humbly show the love of Jesus.

2

"I'VE TROUBLES EVERYWHERE"
The Answer—Solution-centered Prayers

Years ago my wife and I learned an important secret that had to do with prayer. We learned that the length of a prayer does not necessarily determine the degree of help one receives. We learned that many people spend an hour or two a day in prayer, but at the end they have made no progress whatever. This may be because they deal principally with their problems in their prayers. They should be visualizing solutions. This, I believe, is true Bible praying.

One day a very sincere woman came to us, inquiring how many problems she should pray about at one time. We suggested that she think about just one for a period of perhaps one week, but that this one be solution-centered, not problem-centered, except as enough time was taken to identify the problem. As soon as she had diagnosed the situation, she should at once pray about the solution, not the problem. This is in keeping with the Word of God. The Bible does not say to give much thought to problems.

Some people seem to have a version of 2 Peter 1:5-7 that goes something like this: "To your problem of why you doubt, add that of why you are so impure in your thinking. Then add to this impurity of thought the problem Why do I know so little? Add to that the problem of why you have so many bad habits. Add to that the problem Why do I lose my temper? Then add the thought Why am I so irreligious at times? To this add the question Why am I so mean at home? And then add to this the problem Why am I so uncharitable?"

No! No! God tells us to concentrate on the positive traits of the Christlike life. So we should pray about the good we need, not about the bad we have. God's way of praying is solution-centered. We present it in this lesson.

1. *We Gradually Become Like That on Which Our Minds Dwell.* "We all . . . beholding . . . are changed into the same image" (2 Cor. 3:18). "For as he thinketh in his heart, so is he" (Prov. 23:7).

A group of psychiatrists did extensive research on suicide. It is reported that all but one of them committed suicide.

When I was in grammar school a neighbor boy became adept at mimicking a fellow pupil who stammered. Years later we met the mimicker again. He was himself a confirmed stammerer.

The story is told about a minister, a very eloquent speaker, who walked with a slight limp. A young minister who was under the training of this older man was deeply impressed with his character and ministry, and determined to become like this great man. It was later observed that the young minister had not only acquired some of the speaking patterns of the elderly minister, but he also walked with a limp.

2. *The Holy Scriptures Teach Us to Think on Positive Things.* "Whatsoever things are honest, whatsoever things are just . . . whatsoever things are of good report; if there be any virtue, and if there be any praise, think on these things . . . and the God of peace shall be with you" (Phil. 4:8, 9).

When I was learning to ride a bicycle as a lad, I was fearful lest I ride into a tree or utility pole. I glued my eyes on a tree and ran straight into it. Then I glued my eyes on a pole and smashed into it. My older brother, Lane, came to my rescue. He gave me a simple principle: Look where you want to go, and not where you do not want to go. "Look straight down the right lane of the road," said he, "and you will go there." I did. I never again ran into a tree or pole.

A friend of ours went to seek counsel of a professional man who insisted that she "talk out" her problem over an extended period of time. When she was through, he frankly counseled her to commit herself immediately to a mental institution. As she stepped into her car afterward, she exclaimed to her husband, "That fellow is crazier than I!" She then went to a good medical doctor who presented to her the possibility of healing. This gave her new hope. Today she is a good wife and mother, in average health, and doing gospel work in which many souls are blessed.

A happily married couple were advised by a friend that something serious could take place unless they studied the faults of each other and then "talked them out." They had been looking at each other's virtues. Now they followed his counsel and watched for the faults appearing in each other. The next time they saw their friend they were on the verge of divorce. They decided that the first method was better—that of looking at each other's good qualities.

A minister friend of ours is often invited to help restore marital harmony. In his counseling he chats individually with each marriage partner, quietly and diplomatically drawing out from each one the good, worthy qualities and habits of the other. Then tenderly and wisely he enlists the attention of each to dwell on these lovely qualities. He has been used of the Lord to effect many reconciliations.

Before he officiates at a wedding he follows the same principle of encouraging each partner to look for good qualities in the other. He even secures their pledge to do so. According to the latest report, there has not been one divorce among couples he married.

3. Before Any of Us Had a Problem, a Solution Was Already in Existence. Before we sinned, there was a Saviour. Jesus is "the Lamb slain from the foundation of the world" (Rev. 13:8).

Before death, there was life. Before sorrow, there was happiness.

4. For Every Problem We Have, There Is a Solution Awaiting Our Acceptance. This Is True Because the Solutions Are Christ-centered. Peace is offered to the troubled. "Peace I leave with you, my peace I give unto you" (John 14:27). This peace is to those who are Christ-centered—solution-centered. "Thou wilt keep him in perfect peace, whose mind is stayed on thee" (Isa. 26:3). This promise is to those whose mind is *stayed* on Christ. The reason so many do not find that peace is because their minds are stayed on dear self.

The filling of every need is promised. "My God shall supply all your need" (Phil. 4:19).

The problem of being lost has a solution. "Look unto me, and be ye saved, all the ends of the earth: for I am God, and there is none else" (Isa. 45:22).

For sin there is forgiveness and cleansing; for death there is eternal life. These are all promised to the believing, confessing sinner. "If we confess our sins, he is faithful and just to forgive us our sins, and to cleanse us from all unrighteousness." "And this is the promise that he hath promised us, even eternal life" (1 John 1:9; 2:25).

5. Solution-centered Praying Is Scientific Praying. Solution-centered praying is scientific, because in it there is identification of the problem, a recognition of the promises, and application of the particular promises to the problem to test them.

A centurion asked Jesus to heal his servant. Notice his solution-centered prayer: "But speak the word only, and my servant shall be healed" (Matt. 8:8). Jesus replied, "As thou hast believed, so be it done unto thee" (verse 13).

The woman with the issue of blood was solution-centered. If I may touch but His clothes, I shall be healed, she thought. Touching Him, "she felt in her body that she was healed of that plague" (Mark 5:29). Jesus said, "Daughter, thy faith hath made thee whole; go in peace, and be whole of thy plague" (verse 34).

Jacob teaches us not to mull over problems; he became solution-centered. When he feared Esau would slay him, he identified his problem, and immediately claimed two solution-filled promises of his Lord (Gen. 32:9-12). The promises he claimed are found in Genesis 28:13-15, and 31:3.

Jacob then planned his action in harmony with the promises he had claimed. He sent 580 animals ahead of him as gifts to Esau and instructed his servants to refer to him as Esau's "servant." These two solution-centered actions would aid Esau to realize that Jacob was neither returning home as a beggar, nor to lord it over him. Jacob was highly successful (see Genesis 33).

King Jehoshaphat also teaches us not to mull over problems, but to act in harmony with God's promises in faith.

In his prayer he identified his problem, recorded in three verses of Scripture, 2 Chronicles 20:10-12. He also prayed a three-part prayer such as this course teaches: (1) He asked (verse 4); (2) he believed (verse 20); (3) he returned thanks that he had already received by having his army choir sing the victory song before there was the slightest sign of victory (verse 21). His victory was so fabulous it took three days to gather the spoil (verse 22-25).

6. Try a Simple Scientific ABC Solution-centered Prayer of Reception. After identifying the problem, claim the Bible promises as solutions. For many this has proven to be wonderfully effective. We receive letters from many parts of the world containing thrilling experiences growing out of such claims.

First step: Ask.

As you go through the simple ABC prayer method, think of the problem as being at your right, and the solution as being at your left. Think of yourself, as you vocalize your request, as turning toward the solution. Where is your back? Toward the problem. You have not ignored its existence. Rather, once having recognized and identified it, you have begun looking toward the promised solution. Now you need no longer mull over the problem or go first to one person and then another, covering the case history repeatedly. Instead you begin talking about the promised solution.

Second Step: Believe.

Picture yourself moving in the direction of the promised solution. Vocalize your faith by saying, "Lord, I believe." As you, in imagination, move in the direction of the solution you may not be able to fully discern it. But you move in that direction by continually voicing your belief in God and in His promised gift. Keep right on voicing this faith. Keep right on moving even though you see no sign of the solution you have been moving toward. Remember that "faith is . . . the evidence of things not seen" (Heb. 11:1). The promise contains the gift. Your faith in this promise is most pleasing to God. He is delighted (see Heb. 11:6).

Third Step: Claim, or Receive.

Claim the solution promised just as you actually take hold of your luggage at the baggage claim. Is it eternal life you are claiming? Then do what you have been taught to do: "Lay hold on eternal life" (1 Tim. 6:12).

Do you need wisdom? Wisdom "is a tree of life to them that lay hold upon her" (Prov. 3:18).

Is it light you need? Put "on the armour of light" (Rom. 13:12). Is it healing? Then touch "the hem of his garment" (Matt 9:20). It is a new concept to those who have been taught that the way to find solutions is to be problem-centered. But, remember, you cannot see the Statue of Liberty by gazing toward Alcatraz.

Study Guide 2

A Personal Message

Because you may soon be visiting people who do not know Jesus, we briefly mention some principles of getting through to them. You need to be able to tell them of:

The Joy of Jesus. Recently, a woman asked us an important question: "Just *how* would you approach a young man who has lost his way?"

In offering an answer, we would like to think of what Jesus would do, how He would speak and how He would act. Many people have the impression that He was not a happy Man. They overlook such statements of Scripture as: "In thy presence is fulness of joy" (Ps. 16:11); "The joy of the Lord is your strength" (Neh. 8:10); "Restore unto me the joy of thy salvation. . . . Then will I teach transgressors thy ways; and sinners shall be converted unto thee" (Ps. 51:12, 13).

Perhaps one of the main deterrents to youth accepting Christianity has been the solemn, sad countenances of those senior Christians who trained them. Their faces, their conversation, and their lives may have shown youth nothing to cause them to believe that Christianity had answers to life's problems. The very ones who have sought to help young people have often turned them off.

Our Lord made everything to produce "after its kind." A person converted by Jesus Christ and the Holy

Spirit will be a joyful, vibrant, happy convert. And those he introduces to Jesus should become the same.

When in committed faith we claim Christ's promises, our joy is fulfilled as they are granted (see John 16:24).

We must tell them of—

The Unpushy Christ. The notion that we must pressure others to do right is anti-Christian. Our Lord does not push. He invited: "If any man . . . open the door, I will come in to him, and will sup with him, and he with me" (Rev. 3:20); "Whosoever will, let him take the water of life freely" (chap. 22:17); "Choose you . . . whom ye will serve" (Joshua 24:15).

Christ invites. He does not pressure. He answers when men ask (see Matt. 7:7). He doesn't force instruction on anyone. He inspires others to ask Him by asking them.

It is a great art to work as Christ worked; that is, not to force instruction on anyone, but to do things to cause them to ask. Then, when the answer is given, it makes an impression never to be forgotten.

We must tell them about—

Christ's Faith. "Follow me, and I will make you fishers of men," Jesus said (Matt. 4:19). By saying this Jesus expressed His faith in men who, until then, had caught only fish! His faith in them was rewarded. They baptized 3,000 souls in one day under guidance of the Holy Spirit (see Acts 2:41).

To speak doubtfully of people is to encourage the very reaction we seek to prevent. Christ's faith in erring men was so great that He showed He would trust them to tell of Himself to the entire world (Matt. 28:18-20). Let us speak out our confidence in the presence of those we seek to help. Never speak doubtingly of their sincerity. "Honour all men" (1 Peter 2:17); "Speak evil of no man" (Titus 3:2).

We must help them understand—

Christ's Selfless Love. "And now abideth faith, hope, charity [love] . . . but the greatest of these is charity" (1 Cor. 13:13). "With lovingkindness have I drawn thee" (Jer. 31:3). "I drew them . . . with bands of love" (Hosea 11:4).

The love of the Father and the Son is selfless. Jesus took an interest in the other man's interests.

Selfless love does not try to bribe, saying, "I spent thousands of dollars on your education so now you ought to respect my judgment or feelings." Selfless love says, in effect, "I am interested in your happiness"—and means it. If it is not meant, it is hypocrisy.

We must teach them of—

Christ's Hope-inspiring Attitude. "For thou art my hope, O Lord God" (Ps. 71:5). "We are saved by hope" (Rom. 8:24). "And hope maketh not ashamed; because the love of God is shed abroad in our hearts by the Holy Spirit which is given to us" (chap. 5:5). "Which hope we have as an anchor of the soul, both sure and stedfast" (Heb. 6:19).

By our definition, hope is a blending of faith and love. When we lovingly express faith in another, when we tell him we believe he has a mission in life, when we believe he will yet fulfill that mission—this gives hope. He will probably go to bed that night thinking about this expression of faith in him and his future.

A wife expresses her confidence that the marriage will be highly successful. This may be used mightily to save a marriage. A parent expresses confidence in a son who is a drug addict, that he will yet lead many young people to a Christian way of life. God may use this faith to save him from his addiction.

In every soul there are limitless possibilities. We are

to present to the one we are trying to help, the confidence that these possibilities may be realized in him. This is not to be done in a holier-than-thou manner. ("You can only find such a happy life when you straighten up and behave yourself.") To give hope and yet break Christ's law of humility is to break the whole chain—the seven secrets of beautiful communication.

We must tell them of Christ Himself—

Christ—the Secret of Secrets. "The mystery which hath been hid from ages and from generations . . . which is Christ in you, the hope of glory" (Col. 1:26, 27).

To show faith, hope, and love to a soul who seems beyond hope, one must personally experience the power of God (Rom. 1:16, 17). Without His indwelling presence, we shall use carnal weapons (see 2 Cor. 10:4).

When we prayerfully learn to have the attitude of our Lord Jesus Christ, others will probably be led to us. When one comes and tells us of his problem, we do not concentrate on the problem, we point to the solution.

Quiz

Kindly check or fill in the blanks. The correct answers are given below.

1. Do we solve problems by mulling over them repeatedly? Yes........ No........

2. There are three parts to the Prayer of Reception. The first is summed up in the word "............" (Matt. 7:7).

3. As we fulfill the first part of the Prayer of Reception, what are we to look at? At the problem? .... or at the solution? ....

4. The problem having been identified or diagnosed, the second part to the Prayer of Reception is summed up in the word "............" (Mark 11:24).

5. As we believe, our minds go more and more in the direction of the solution? .... or the problem? ....

6. The third part of the Prayer of Reception is to claim, or "............" (Matt. 21:22).

7. When we thank God that we have received, do we lay hold more tightly on the problem? .... or the solution promised? ....

Correct Answers

1. No
2. ask
3. solution
4. believe

5. solution
6. receive
7. solution

Assignment

We suggest that you drill yourself on the three-step scientific prayer. Practice the plan several times in the period of one week between lessons, and see for yourself what it will do for your life. Also, review several times the section "A Personal Message." This is extremely important, because you will soon be communicating with those for whom you and the Fellowship of Prayer are praying.

3

A DROWNING BROTHER—SAVED
Seven Steps in Saving Your Loved Ones

First Step: Beholding Christ Ourselves. "I saw also the Lord sitting upon a throne, high and lifted up, and his train filled the temple" (Isa. 6:1). "Suddenly there shone from heaven a great light round about me and I fell unto the ground, and heard a voice saying unto me, Saul, Saul, why persecutest thou me?" (Acts 22:6, 7). "God forbid that I should glory, save in the cross of our Lord Jesus Christ" (Gal. 6:14).

A little 6-year-old lad was listening to his mother tell the story of Jesus as she swept his bedroom. It was the sweetest, most glorious story he had ever heard. Using the simplest language, she described His life, from the time the little stars twinkled over Bethlehem at His birth, until His cruel trials, His walk to Calvary, and His humiliating death. She told her little son that Jesus did all of this for sinners, including him.

Second Step: Claiming Forgiveness. "Then said I, Woe is me! for I am undone; because I am a man of unclean lips . . . for mine eyes have seen the King, the Lord of hosts. Then flew one of the seraphims unto me . . . and said . . . thine iniquity is taken away, and thy sin purged" (Isa. 6:5-7). "This a faithful saying, and worthy of all acceptation, that Christ Jesus came into the world to save sinners; of whom I am chief" (1 Tim. 1:15).

The lad, his heart breaking in repentance and his

eyes wet with tears, asked his mother what to do. She suggested claiming the promise "If we confess our sins, he is faithful and just to forgive us our sins, and to cleanse us from all unrighteousness" (1 John 1:9). He fell on his knees in deep contrition and asked for forgiveness and cleansing. He got up from his knees knowing that he was forgiven.

Third Step: The Call to Share the Knowledge of Jesus. "I heard the voice of the Lord, saying, Whom shall I send, and who will go for us?" (Isa. 6:8). "He is a chosen vessel unto me, to bear my name before the Gentiles, and kings, and the children of Israel" (Acts 9:15).

Two or three years after his conversion experience the lad had a dream in which, standing on the shore, he saw his older brother, Lester, drowning in the ocean. He saw the angry waves wrap around his brother; he could plainly see the distress on his face, the plea to be rescued.

The lad was trembling when he awoke; tears were on his cheeks. Then very clearly he heard a "thought voice." It was the Lord telling him he had many, many brothers and sisters all over the world sinking in sin's ocean. The voice told him to go out and save them from an eternal death. The lad replied that he was totally unable to do this; he could no more do it than he could save his brother from the angry ocean waves. Then the voice of his Lord tenderly assured him that He would teach him, strengthen him, and give him success.

Fourth Step: The Response. "Then said I, Here am I, send me" (Isa. 6:8). "I was not disobedient unto the heavenly vision" (Acts 26:19).

Filled with sweet assurance from his Lord, the lad responded from the very depths of his being, "Lord, depending on You I will go wherever You send me."

Fifth Step: Interceding for Others. "Yet now, if thou wilt forgive their sin—; and if not, blot me, I pray thee, out of thy book which thou hast written" (Ex. 32:32). "I have great heaviness and continual sorrow in my heart. For I could wish that myself were accursed from Christ for my brethren, my kinsmen according to the flesh" (Rom. 9:2, 3). "I exhort therefore, that, first of all supplications, prayers, intercessions, and giving of thanks, be made for all men" (1 Tim. 2:1).

As the lad pondered the mission Heaven had given him and the great sacrifice of his Lord for sinners, he found his heart aching for people—his neighbors and friends. He asked himself a hundred times, How can I help them to be ready to meet the Lord? He prayed, "Lord, help me to help them. I long to be sure they are ready to meet Jesus."

In academy, the maturing lad spent time every morning interceding with the Lord for the people whose names were on his prayer list. One for whom he was praying *was* his brother, Lester, whom he had dreamed was drowning. At the time, Lester was passing through a time of great discouragement.

The brothers were living with their parents near the academy; and so one day when the parents were away and Lester was apparently off someplace struggling with his discouragement, the younger brother decided to pray until Lester found the strength and courage he needed. In his bedroom he fell on his knees and pleaded with all his heart for his brother whom the waves of discouragement might even now be swallowing up. He felt impressed to remain on his knees in earnest prayer. Ten minutes he prayed. Twenty. Thirty. Finally, forty minutes.

Then he heard a sound downstairs. Footsteps were coming through the kitchen, and up the stairway. Then the door opened to his room. His heart almost skipped a beat as Lester knelt by his side. Placing his arm around his praying brother, Lester tearfully asked, "Were you praying for me?"

In holy rapture the brother replied, "Yes, I was, Lester."

Lester's discouragement dissolved. Later he became a mighty preacher and soul winner for the Lord. Can one doubt that the intercession of his brother had a part in this experience?

Sixth Step: Praying With Others For Others. Today that praying younger brother often reads the glorious promise of our Lord: "Again I say unto you, that if two of you shall agree on earth as touching anything that they shall ask, it shall be done for them of my Father which is in heaven. For where two or three are gathered together in my name, there am I in the midst of them" (Matt. 18:19, 20).

Many were the times in school when the young man sought out student friends and retired to a quiet place of prayer. They prayed for themselves and others. Miracles took palce. On one occasion in a young man's prayer group a demon was cast out. What rewarding experiences! What glorious answers!

Seventh Step: Learning to Communicate With Those Interceded For. "The Lord hath given me the tongue of the learned, that I should know how to speak a word in season to him that is weary" (Isa. 50:4). "Brethren, if a man be overtaken in a fault, ye which are spiritual, restore such an one in the spirit of meekness; considering thyself, lest thou also be tempted. Bear ye one another's burdens, and so fulfil the law of Christ" (Gal. 6:1, 2).

Through school, college, and in the ministry, that praying brother has been trying to inspire every Christian to believe that these seven steps will bring a glorious reward indeed.

Quiz

1. Are you experiencing an emptiness in your Christian life? ....
2. Have you wondered why this is so and whether a different, satisfying experience cannot be yours? ....
3. Do you feel helpless to find this experience, and have you a lack of knowledge as to how to seek it? ....
4. Is it your desire to learn how to converse on a spiritual level with those for whom you are burdened and to pray so that God can move them to respond in a spiritual way? ....
5. If you have never done so before, will you make a commitment to your Lord to learn, by His help, how to engage in intercessory prayer for those for whom you are burdened? ....
6. Will you make a commitment to learn and follow the science of soul-winning communication so you can get through to the hearts of others? ....

Assignment

1. Prayerfully review the lesson three times.
2. Prayerfully contact another person of your own sex, inviting him or her to follow this series of lessons with you. If some whom you contact show no interest, do not pressure them. Try to find someone who is *in trouble* and comfort him. Then invite him, or her, to meet with you once a week in this series of studies.
3. Go back over the seven steps in the foregoing Lesson Guide and study them very carefully.

4

SINCERE SINNERS
Why Christians Misunderstand Them

Our Lord Sees, Hears, and Wants to Loose. "For the
Lord seeth not as man seeth; for man looketh on the
outward appearance, but the Lord looketh on the heart"
(1 Sam. 16:7). Jesus "needed not that any should testify
of man: for he knew what was in man" (John 2:25). God
"hath looked down from the height of his sanctuary;
from heaven did the Lord behold the earth; to hear the
groaning of the prisoner; to loose those that are ap-
pointed to death" (Ps. 102:19, 20).

There are several types of unconverted people we
might call "sincere sinners":

1. The Masked Antagonist. "I verily thought with
myself, that I ought to do many things contrary to the
name of Jesus of Nazareth" (Acts 26:9), Paul wrote,
describing himself at one stage of his experience.

Sinners sometimes give the appearance that they
cannot be touched with religion. They wear a mask that
tempts the Christian to think it is hopeless to try to
bring them to Christ. But often beneath the mask there
is "the groaning of the prisoner" that God has heard,
and they can be changed.

A bitter antagonist came to our meetings determined to stir up strife. God helped us to turn from our
natural inclination to "put him in his place" to show
tenderness instead. The result was that before the week
ended he had given himself to Christ in deep repent-

ance. He found forgiveness, cleansing, and eternal life as promised in 1 John 1:9 and 2:25.

2. The Apparently Unconcerned May Be Masked. During one series of meetings that we were conducting, we learned of a man and wife who no longer attended church because of some controversy. Though we did not know them, we went to their home and apologized for any coldness on the part of the church. We did not tell them that *they* were right. We only confessed our faults as commanded by our Lord (James 5:16). Both returned to church. They were very happy that we had come humbly to their home.

3. The Flippant. A girl at a college where I pastored appeared extremely irreligious. As I began my ministry at the college I felt impressed to reveal the humble love of our Lord. I prayed to be able to do this in my sermons and personal visits, although I am sure I sometimes failed in this respect. After six weeks this girl came to my study for an interview. She told me that at the very time she appeared so frivolous and flippant she *often* went to her dormitory room, flung herself on her bed, and sobbed out her agony of spirit. Sometimes she wept for an hour, sometimes two hours. She told me she dared not look up to God in prayer, for she was too unworthy. After her cry she would bathe her face, go out on the campus, and assume her frivolous attitude again. Learning during that six weeks that our Lord's love does not condemn, scold, or belittle, but freely forgives, she dared to come to the pastor's study. There I taught her how she could ask, believe, and receive the promised forgiveness and cleansing, and eternal life (1 John 1:9; 2:25).

There Is Converting Power in Our Lord's Promises: "Whereby are given unto us exceeding great and precious promises: that by these ye might be partakers of the divine nature, having escaped the corruption that is in the world through lust" (2 Peter 1:4); "Having therefore these promises, dearly beloved, let us cleanse ourselves from all filthiness of the flesh and spirit, perfecting holiness in the fear of God" (2 Cor. 7:1).

There Are Things for Us to Do to Cooperate So Hearts Will Open to the Promises of God: "Go home to thy friends, and tell them how great things the Lord hath done for thee, and hath had compassion on thee" (Mark 5:19); "This book of the law shall not depart out of thy mouth; but thou shalt meditate therein day and night, that thou mayest observe to do according to all that is written therein: for then thou shalt make thy way prosperous, and then thou shalt have good success" (Joshua 1:8); "A word fitly spoken is like apples of gold in pictures of silver" (Prov. 25:11).

Assignment and Quiz

We suggest that each student prayerfully ask himself, To what extent am I observing the following simple principles? When weaknesses are seen, ask the Lord for help in correcting them.

1. Am I a good listener, or do I have a tendency to monopolize the conversation? ....
   "He wakeneth my ear to *hear* as the learned" (Isa. 50:4).

2. Do I try to win arguments, or am I willing to have a winning attitude of love?
   "Do all things without murmurings and disputings" (Phil. 2:14).

3. Do I have an attitude of condemnation toward those whom I know are doing wrong, or do I let the Holy Spirit do the convicting while I remain sweet and calm? ....
   "God sent not his son into the world to condemn the world" (John 3:17). "And when he [the Holy Spirit] is come, he will reprove the world of sin" (chap. 16:8). "In quietness and confidence shall be your strength" (Isa. 30:15).

4. Am I inclined to belittle a person for a vice, perhaps to shame him into reform, or do I pray for him, claiming the presence of the Holy Spirit to give him a power for victory that I cannot give him? ....
   "Esteem other better than [yourselves]" (Phil. 2:3). "Not by might, nor by power, but by my spirit, saith the Lord" (Zech. 4:6).

5. Do I find myself criticizing others instead of looking for the good in them? ....
   "Speak evil of no man" (Titus 3:2).

6. Am I inclined to think that some faulty person should apologize to me or to the church, or have I begun obeying the command of the Lord to "confess your faults one to another" (James 5:16)? ....

Lesson Guide

5

"HALLELUJAH, $6,000!"
Rejoicing in the Science of Prayer

At one time in our experience we were in a very tight situation, needing $6,000 to make a payment on a farm. We had not wanted a farm, only a place in the country with sufficient land for a garden. But after searching for weeks, we found nothing like what we wanted. However, in answer to special prayer, and by a series of what I see as miracles, we were led to buy a farm, with the idea of sharing acreage with others who wanted to move out of the city. God's answer to our need for money caused us to exclaim, "Hallelujah, a $6,000 answer!"

By that experience we learned principles that apply to every area of life. Let us share this science with you.

1. Science Suggests Knowledge. The first word in my dictionary defining science is "knowledge." It means "to know." The apostle John tells us about the knowledge that makes prayer scientific. "And this is the confidence that we have in him, that, if we ask any thing according to his will, he heareth us: and if we know that he hear us, whatsoever we ask, we know that we have the petitions that we desired of him" (1 John 5:14, 15). Not that we *might* have, or *would like to have,* but actually *have.*

2. The Basis of This Knowledge Is a Simple Seed. "A sower went out to sow his seed" (Luke 8:5). "The seed is the word of God" (verse 11).

A girl in British Columbia, Canada, was showing a grapefruit to friends, including some members of our team. We saw that the grapefruit was open, and a seed was exposed. The seed itself had also opened, and we could see what looked like a tiny grapefruit tree coming right out of that cracked seed. The tiny "tree" had two leaves, a trunk, and a root.

Rutherford Platt, a prize winner in science, expressed the opinion that every normal apple seed contains three parts of an apple tree—a trunk, two leaves, and roots. He stated that this tree could actually be seen if one used a magnifying glass large enough.

A friend of ours took us to a place where there were wild persimmons. When we found them, he told us to cut one of the seeds slantwise. There we saw what suggested to us a persimmon tree, tiny, but with trunk, leaves, and roots.

What is true of a grapefruit seed, an apple seed, and a persimmon seed is also true of other seeds. Every normal acorn, for instance, contains a potential oak tree.

In a parable that He told, Jesus likened Scriptures to seed (see Luke 8:11). Every Bible promise, being the Word of God, is seed, and it is said that there are at least 3,573 promises, or clusters of promises, in the Bible.

3. Each Bible Promise Contains, as It Were, the Thing It Names. An apple seed promises an apple tree—and it also potentially contains one. A grapefruit seed promises a grapefruit tree, so it may be thought of as containing a grapefruit tree.

A Bible promise for wisdom is a seed that contains wisdom. "If any of you lack wisdom . . . it shall be given him" (James 1:5).

A Bible promise for light contains light. "I will make darkness light . . ." (Isa. 42:16).

A Bible promise for peace contains peace. "My peace I give unto you" (John 14:27).

4. *To Activate the Seed, We Must Have Faith.* "Let us therefore fear, lest, a promise being left us of entering into his rest, any of you should seem to come short of it. . . . But the word preached did not profit them, not being mixed with faith" (Heb. 4:1, 2).

Years ago an Eastern monarch's tomb that had been sealed shut for centuries was discovered and opened. Inside were found some poppy seeds. Placed in soil, exposed to moisture and the warmth of sunlight, they germinated. They grew. They bloomed.

Part of the science of prayer is to claim Bible promises. Each promise contains what is promised, as it were. The gift is in the promise. If we receive a promise, and have the faith to claim it, we will have the gift promised.

5. *Jesus Declared That Prayer Must Be Based on His Word.* "If ye abide in me, and my words abide in you, ye shall ask what ye will, and it shall be done unto you" (John 15:7).

The science of prayer, therefore, is based on two things: Our abiding in Christ, and His abiding in us. Please read it again: "If ye abide in me, and my words abide in you, ye shall ask what ye will, and it shall be done unto you."

The main reason for our not accepting at full face value such fabulous promises as "Ask what ye will" has been that we have not known that the prayer of faith must be based on what God has promised. We must ask for what God has promised and then use what we receive in advancing His cause.

6. *Summarizing:*

a. Part of the science of prayer is to know God keeps His promises (1 John 5:15).

b. The Word of God is seed; therefore, every promise in the Bible contains the gift promised (Luke 8:11).

c. True scientific prayer is based on Bible promises (2 Peter 3:9).

d. We add here the thought that we are not merely to ask and believe, but to *return thanks that we have been heard by God.* (John 11:41).

Study Guide 5

A Personal Message

Jesus is the example for the Christian in his conversation as in everything else. What did Jesus talk about? The answer is very simple. When He met a man who had leprosy, He talked about cleansing (see Matt. 8:2, 3). When He met men who were fishermen, He discussed fishing (see John 21:5, 6). Jesus did not talk about fishing to a man who needed cleansing from leprosy. Neither did He discuss leprosy with the men whose primary interest was fishing. He met men where they were. He conversed with them concerning things in which they were interested.

Here is an important lesson for many would-be soul winners: Discover the interests of the individual with whom you chat. Then visit about that interest if it is a legitimate, pure, moral one.

People are seldom repelled by a conversation when we speak about things in which they are interested. Much of Christ's ministry was made up of this kind of communication.

If the one we visit has a child who is ill, he is interested in that child. If we would gain his interest, if we would follow the example of Jesus, we will talk about the restoration of that child. Pray for the child. Ask God to heal him. If he is interested in a big catch of fish, talk about fishing. You may learn something from him concerning how to catch souls and at the same time get through to him for Christ.

Quiz

Why not fill in the blanks below, and check them according to the answers given at the bottom of the page.

1. The term *science* means "............ ...."
2. In Christ's parable of the seeds, the seed is the .... of God (Luke 8:11).
3. Therefore every Bible promise is a ....
4. Every promise in the Bible contains the .... promised.
5. A promise for wisdom contains ....
6. A promise for peace contains ....
7. A promise for light contains ....
8. In order to activate Bible promises in our personal lives we must mix them with .... (Heb. 4:2).
9. When we have learned the true science of prayer, we will be able to say, "we .... that we have the petitions that we desired of him" (1 John 5:15).
10. Every scientific prayer must be based on a Bible ....
11. Jesus taught us to .... (Matt. 7:7).
12. He commanded us to .... (Mark 11:24).
13. He told us that we would then .... (Matt. 21:22).

Correct Answers

1. to know
2. word
3. seed
4. gift
5. wisdom
6. peace
7. light

8. faith
9. know
10. promise
11. ask
12. believe
13. receive

Assignment

If you have not yet participated in a prayer fellow-ship, we suggest that you either begin one or partici-pate in one this week. It will do your soul good. Why wait any longer when Jesus our Lord has so strongly given us this pattern of sharing our faith in Him?

We believe that Jesus Christ is our pattern in soul winning. He knows how to get through to the human heart.

Review several times the "Personal Message" sec-tion (Page 53). Prayerfully ask the Lord to help you to try Christ's methods as you implore the Holy Spirit to give you wisdom for the most rewarding undertaking suggested there (Luke 11:13; James 1:5).

Lesson Guide

6

WHEN EVERYTHING WENT WRONG
Cross-examined in Heaven's Court

When we received glorious answers to our prayers in connection with the $6,000 we referred to in the previous study, we were overjoyed. We told the seller of the farm we intended to tell people everywhere about the goodness of our Lord.

After we have testified to our Lord's goodness, everything seemed to go wrong, physically, emotionally, and otherwise. Then I made the mistake of complaining, not directly against the Lord, but against circumstances. I forgot that Satan demands his turn. He demands the right to cross-examine us. And then he contends we will change our testimony of God's goodness. I became so exhausted that my ministry seemed to be closing. Then I began praising the Lord with all my heart. The result was that healing came to my body, soul, and mind.

1. We Are to Be Witnesses to Our Friends and Loved Ones. "Go home to thy friends, and tell them how great things the Lord hath done for thee, and hath had compassion on thee" (Mark 5:19). "Ye are my witnesses, saith the Lord" (Isa. 43:10). "Ye shall receive power, after that the Holy Ghost is come upon you: and ye shall be witnesses unto me" (Acts 1:8).

2. We Are Witnesses to the Unseen Universe. "For we are made a spectacle unto the world, and to *angels*"

(1 Cor. 4:9). "To the intent that now unto the *principalities and powers in heavenly places* might be known by the church the manifold wisdom of God, according to the eternal purpose which he purposed in Christ Jesus our Lord" (Eph. 3:10, 11).

3. Satan Claims That We Will Change Our Testimony as to God's Love and Care When We Are Cross-examined by Affliction, Trouble, and Trial. "And he shewed me Joshua the high priest standing before the angel of the Lord, and Satan standing at his right hand to resist him" (Zech. 3:1). "Then Satan answered the Lord, and said, Doth Job fear God for nought? . . . But put forth thine hand now, and touch all that he hath, and he will curse thee to thy face" (Job 1:9-11).

4. Our Lord, Mediator, and Advocate Expects Us Not to Change Our Testimony to His Goodness Under Satan's Attacks. "Be thou faithful unto death, and I will give thee a crown of life" (Rev. 2:10). "Howbeit for this cause I obtained mercy, that in me first Jesus Christ might shew forth all longsuffering, for a pattern to them which should hereafter believe on him to life everlasting" (1 Tim. 1:16). "Do all things without murmurings and disputings: that ye may be blameless and harmless, the sons of God, without rebuke, in the midst of a crooked and perverse nation, among whom ye shine as lights in the world" (Phil. 2:14, 15). "My brethren, count it all joy when ye fall into divers temptations" (James 1:2).

5. Especially Are We in the Last-Day Conflict to Praise God and Not Change Our Testimony. "And the dragon was wroth with the woman, and went to make war with the remnant of her seed, which keep the commandments of God, and have the testimony of

Jesus Christ" (Rev. 12:17). "The accuser of our brethren is cast down, which accused them before our God day and night. And they overcame him by the blood of the Lamb, and by the word of their testimony; and they loved not their lives unto the death. Therefore rejoice, ye heavens, and ye that dwell in them" (verses 10-12). "But of the times and the seasons, brethren, ye have no need that I write unto you. For yourselves know perfectly that the day of the Lord so cometh as a thief in the night. . . . But ye, brethren, are not in darkness, that that day should overtake you as a thief. Ye are the children of light, and the children of the day." "Rejoice evermore. . . . In every thing give thanks" (1 Thess. 5:1-5, 16-18).

6. Calvary Love Is the Basis of Our Unchanging Testimony. "And we know that all things work together for good to them that love God, to them who are the called according to his purpose. . . . He that spared not his own Son, but delivered him up for us all, how shall he not with him also freely give us all things? . . . Who is he, that condemneth? It is Christ that died, yea rather, that is risen again, who is even at the right hand of God, who also maketh intercession for us. . . . For I am persuaded, that neither death, nor life, nor angels, nor principalities, nor powers, nor things to come, Nor height, nor depth, nor any other creature, shall be able to separate us from the love of God, which is in Christ Jesus our Lord" (Rom. 8:28-39).

7. God Rewards Our Unchanging Testimony. "And the Lord said unto Satan, Behold, all that he hath is in thy power" (Job 1:12). (Please read verses 13-20 to see the havoc Satan wrought upon Job.)

"And [Job] said . . . the Lord gave, and the Lord hath taken away; blessed be the name of the Lord. In all this Job sinned not, nor charged God foolishly" (verses 21,

22). "What? shall we receive good at the hand of God, and shall we not receive evil? In all this did not Job sin with his lips" (chap. 2:10). "Though he slay me, yet will I trust in him" (chap. 13:15). "So the Lord blessed the latter end of Job more than his beginning" (chap. 42:12).

8. If We Fail to Testify for God, Satan Has an Advantage Over Us.
"And the people spake against God, and against Moses. . . . And the Lord sent fiery serpents among the people, and they bit the people; and much people of Israel died" (Num. 21:5, 6). "Because thou servedst not the Lord thy God with joyfulness, and with gladness of heart, for the abundance of things; therefore shalt thou serve thine enemies which the Lord shall send against thee . . . until he have destroyed thee" (Deut. 28:47, 48). "Because that, when they knew God, they glorified him not as God, neither were thankful . . . their foolish heart was darkened" (Rom. 1:21).

9. If We Repent of Our Changed Testimony, God Will Freely Forgive.
"Therefore the people came to Moses, and said, We have sinned, for we have spoken against the Lord, and against thee; pray unto the Lord, that he take away the serpents from us. And Moses prayed for the people. And the Lord said unto Moses, Make thee a fiery serpent, and set it upon a pole: and it shall come to pass, that every one that is bitten, when he looketh upon it, shall live" (Num. 21:7, 8). "Wherefore have we fasted, say they, and thou seest not? wherefore have we afflicted our soul, and thou takest no knowledge? . . . Is it such a fast that I have chosen? a day for a man to afflict his soul? . . . Is not this the fast that I have chosen? to loose the bands of wickedness, to undo the heavy burdens? . . . Then shall thy light break forth as the morning, and thine health shall spring forth speedily. . . . Then shalt thou call, and the Lord shall answer; thou

shalt cry, and he shall say, Here I am. . . . And the Lord shall guide thee continually" (Isa. 58:3-11).

10. Our Testimony of Praise to God Will Have a Converting Power Over Others: "Restore unto me the joy of thy salvation; and uphold me with thy free spirit. Then will I teach transgressors thy ways; and sinners shall be converted unto thee" (Ps. 51:12, 13).

Bring peace of mind: "Rejoice in the Lord, alway: and again I say, Rejoice. . . . And the peace of God, which passeth all understanding, shall keep your hearts and minds through Christ Jesus" (Phil. 4:4-7).

Bring us strength: "The joy of the Lord is your strength" (Neh. 8:10).

Develop patience and true Christian experience: "My brethren, count it all joy when ye fall into divers temptation; knowing this, that the trying of your faith worketh patience. But let patience have her perfect work, that ye may be perfect and entire, wanting nothing" (James 1:2-4); "Here is the patience of the saints" (Rev. 14:12).

Promote physical strength: "Bless the Lord, O my soul: and all that is within me, bless his holy name. Bless the Lord, O my soul, and forget not all his benefits: who forgiveth all thine iniquities; who healeth all thy diseases; who redeemeth thy life from destruction; who crowneth thee with lovingkindness and tender mercies; who satisfieth thy mouth with good things; so that thy youth is renewed like the eagle's" (Ps. 103:1-5).

Study Guide 6

A Personal Message

When prayer partners visit a sin-burdened soul, it should be without a condemning spirit. No criticism should be in their conversation with respect to dear ones who have lost their way, or in regard to the church or its members.

Probably one of the prime factors for young people leaving the church is a negative, critical, complaining attitude of older members. Let us ask our Lord to forgive us for any negative attitude we might have and to make us praising, rejoicing children of His, even under the most crushing circumstances.

Quiz

1. We are .... for the Lord (Isa. 43:10).
2. We are to witness, not merely to the inhabitants of earth, but to .... (1 Cor. 4:9).
3. Satan claims we will .... God if we are afflicted (Job 1:9-12)
4. Our Lord commands us to do all things without .... and .... (Phil. 2:14).
5. The church of the last days is to rejoice .... (1 Thess. 5:16).
6. When we respond to Calvary love, we can testify that .... things work together for good to us (Rom. 8:28).

7. God rewarded Job for not changing his testimony under great difficulty and suffering by blessing him at the close more than at the .... (Job 42:12).
8. If we let the Lord restore to us the joy of His salvation, sinners will be .... unto Him (Ps. 51:12, 13).
9. A merry heart does good like a .... (Prov. 17:22).
10. If we rejoice in the Lord continually, He will give us .... (Phil. 4:4-7).

Correct Answers
1. witnesses
2. angels
3. curse
4. murmurings, disputings
5. evermore
6. all
7. beginning
8. converted
9. medicine
10. peace

Lesson Guide **7**

A GREAT DISTRESS

"No, Mother—Not an Infidel!"

When my wife and I began claiming Bible promises in a way we had not done before, we were immediately challenged. Two of my brothers frankly told us they doubted we had received answers from God. They thought we were guilty of presumption.

We felt that much was at stake. If my brothers had properly evaluated the situation, we should be willing to confess at once that we were mistaken. On the other hand, if we were truly exercising faith, we should move forward.

Of one thing we were certain—we did not deserve any answers. But could we, unworthy though we were, claim with certainty the promises of the Bible? Were the promises meant for us today, under all circumstances and in all walks of life? We had to know.

To clarify our thinking, we wrote down several questions and their answers, which we placed on the flyleaves of our Bibles. We referred to them often so that we might drill ourselves on the points made. We suggest that you follow the same procedure. The questions and answers followed more or less this outline:

1. How Do You Know There Is a God? One of our brothers had a sermon titled, "How I Convince the Infidel There Is a God." It contained beautiful experiences that demonstrated God's existence. The evidence was drawn chiefly from nature. My brother had investigated extensively into various facets of nature that he drew from to prove that a mind controls it. He showed in a convincing way that from the time a seed of any kind is planted, until it germinates, springs from the ground, develops, and bears its blooms or its fruit, it is controlled by law. It has order. It has beauty. It reveals design. It shows that a mind controls it with a means to an end. He summed up this portion of his sermon with the statement: "The law, the beauty, the order, the symmetry, the design, the means to an end in all created works, postulates mind. There is nothing in our planet that reveals these characteristics where a mind is not involved. Even a humble, unattractive traffic light suggests that some mind put it there. How much more the works of nature."

I had heard that a tiny flower had been used of God to convert a criminal behind bars. I picked up a blossom and observed its beauty, its symmetry, its design. I saw that the laws of life controlled it. It had order and means to an end from the time it was a seed until its day was done.

Then I looked up into the vast vault of blue. I had loved to study astronomy. With the psalmist I could cry out, "The heavens declare the glory of God; and the firmament sheweth his handywork" (Ps. 19:1). "The fool hath said in his heart, There is no God" (Ps. 14:1).

2. How Do We Know God Is Wise Enough to Solve Our Problems? This was the next question in our outline. Wisdom was seen in the germination of the little flower in its development from its first day to its full blooming. I thought of all the intricacies of nature, and I could say, "He hath established the world by his wisdom" (Jer. 10:12). A profound proof!

3. How Do We Know God Is Powerful Enough to Solve Our Problems? This was our next question. We needed a God, not merely one who existed, but one who was wise enough and powerful enough to solve the problems we faced. We reviewed astronomy, and thought of the runaway speed of Arcturus. Arcturus is but one among the billions of suns within billions of universes. Surely "he hath made the earth by his power" (Jer. 10:12). And the "heavens" are the "work of thy fingers" (Ps. 8:3). "Yes," I cried, "God is wise enough and powerful enough to handle our problems." But we needed another question answered.

4. Is God Personally Interested in an Unimportant Creature Such as I? Again I looked at the tiny flower. I saw my answer in it. God made this flower—only a dot as compared to me—perfect. It was beautiful—perfectly beautiful. God had a personal interest in that speck of a flower, from the moment it was a seed and all through its development.

"Wherefore, if God so clothe the grass of the field, which today is, and tomorrow is cast into the oven" (Matt. 6:30), shall He not much more take a personal interest in my problems? Yes, a thousand times, yes. That silent flower spoke eloquently of our heavenly Father's care.

5. How Do You Know God Communicates to Us Personally in the Bible? We pondered on how completely foolish it would be to think of an infinitely wise, powerful, loving God unable to communicate to the intelligent creatures He had made. We outlined three evidences of His communication to mankind in the Bible.

First, we recalled the various prophecies of the Bible we had presented in our public ministry over the years. They had, without exception, been fulfilled as God said. There were no crystal-ball errors such as our modern "prophets" commit.

It is said that of the approximately 1,335 Bible prophecies, 1,000 have already been fulfilled, and not one has failed. We recalled the experience of Josiah Litch and his interpretation of Revelation 9:10-15. From his study of prophecy he predicted, in 1838, that the Turkish Empire would end on August 11, 1840. When events took place that were seen as proving him right, hundreds of atheists and infidels believed. We thought, If, on the basis of one fulfilled prophecy, infidels could accept the Bible as God's communication to man, what about ourselves? We know there are hundreds upon hundreds of fulfilled prophecies. Should not our faith be stronger in the Bible than that of 1,000 unbelievers who were converted on the basis of *one* fulfilled prophecy?

Jesus said, "Now I tell you before it come, that, when it is come to pass, ye may believe that I am he" (John 13:19).

Second, we placed on our outline a list of dramatically changed lives. We listed murderers, adulterers, thieves, proud and arrogant blasphemers. We knew that their lives had been completely changed through their reverent study of the Bible. This is what Bible promises can do. "Whereby are given unto us exceeding great and precious promises: that by these ye might be partakers of the divine nature, having escaped the corruption that is in the world through lust" (2 Peter 1:4).

Third, we had the evidence of our own experience. We placed on our outline what we knew beyond question the Book had done for us. We knew that when we had reverently studied its pages, it had worked a transformation in our lives. When we had neglected its study, our carnal natures had begun to express themselves. What Jesus said is true: "Now ye are clean through the word which I have spoken unto you" (John 15:3).

6. *The Bible Promises Are as Sure as God Himself.* Our conclusion: "By myself have I sworn" (Gen. 22:16). "Wherein God, willing more abundantly to shew unto the heirs of promise the immutability of his counsel, confirmed it by an oath: that by two immutable things, in which it was impossible for God to lie, we might have a strong consolation, who have fled for refuge to lay hold upon the hope set before us: which hope we have as an anchor of the soul, both sure and stedfast, and which entereth into that within the veil" (Heb. 6:17-19).

7. *We Knew That Others Had Come to the Same Conclusion.* Joshua challenged Israel in these words: "Ye know in all your hearts and in all your souls, that not one thing hath failed of all the good things which the Lord your God spake concerning you" (Joshua 23:14).

Samuel declared, "The Strength of Israel will not lie nor repent: for he is not a man, that he should repent" (1 Sam. 15:29).

The psalmist stated, "Thy word is true from the beginning" (Ps. 119:160).

Jeremiah exclaimed, "The Lord is the true God" (Jer. 10:10).

Paul, the apostle, was certain that "all the promises of God in him are yea, and in him Amen, unto the glory of God by us" (2 Cor. 1:20).

Even Balaam, the backslidden prophet of God, cried out, "God is not a man, that he should lie, neither the son of man, that he should repent: hath he said, and shall he not do it? or hath he spoken, and shall he not make it good?" (Num. 23:19).

Victorious souls before God's throne will sing, "Great and marvelous are thy works, Lord God Almighty; just and true are thy ways, thou King of saints" (Rev. 15:3).

One hundred million angels around God's throne cry out, "Worthy is the Lamb that was slain to receive power, and riches, and wisdom, and strength, and honour, and glory, and blessing" (chap. 5:12).

And we cried out, "My heart is fixed, O God, my heart is fixed: I will sing and give praise" (Ps. 57:7).

8. Consequently, We Decided to Accept the Bible Promises as Personal. We prayed before an open Bible as did George Müller, that famous man of prayer. We often took the Bible in our hands and opened it to a promise, as did Monica, mother of Augustine. She placed her fingers right on a promise of God. She made that promise very personal.

We have a personal God. Then, why not accept His promises as being for us, personally?

"If ye be Christ's, then are ye Abraham's seed, and heirs according to the promise" (Gal. 3:29).

C. H. Spurgeon, one of the greatest preachers of all time, once said, "Prayer pulls the rope below, and the great bell rings above in the ears of God. . . . He who wins with heaven is the man who grasps the rope boldly and pulls continuously, with all his might."

Norman Macleod gave this testimony: "There is no such thing in the long history of God's kingdom as an unanswered prayer. Every true desire from a child's heart finds some true answer in the heart of God."

During the many months when my distress was great because of the test we were undergoing, I determined to speak faith, sing faith, and pray prayers of faith.

Mother, hearing my faith being expressed so strongly, was filled with concern. She feared that when I was apparently let down I would hit bottom spiritually in my relationship with the Lord.

"I am afraid you will become an infidel," she commented sadly one day.

"Why do you say that?" I asked.

"Because you are expecting so much," she replied. "When you do not receive it, you will be so disappointed you will turn from God in deep disbelief."

I replied, "No, Mother—not an infidel!"

One of the keys to not being disappointed with God's answers is, We are not to tell God *how* to answer our prayers. Isaiah 42:16 has been our guide through the years as we have asked believingly, always bearing in mind that God reserves to His infinite wisdom the *how* and *when* of answering. "I will bring the blind by a way that they knew not; I will lead them in paths that they have not known: I will make darkness light before them, and crooked things straight. These things will I do unto them, and not forsake them."

A Personal Message

Everywhere there are souls in deep distress. The only way they can find real peace is by believing God and accepting His promises at full value.

As we have shared our experience with you in this study, so you can share your faith experience with others, whatever that may be. If you have had a *battle* of faith, share that. As you tell how the Lord has kept His word to you, how your own distress subsided each time you claimed His promises in simple, childlike faith, it may have a profound influence on another.

Troubled individuals want to know what practical value one's religious beliefs have been to him. Heavy-laden souls do not ask for theories that have not benefited us. They want actual solutions. They want to see that God's promises have been relevant to our own lives.

Quiz

1. "The heavens declare the glory of ...." (Ps. 19:1).
2. "He hath established the world by his ...." (Jer. 10:12).
3. We know God takes a personal interest in every soul because He has clothed the .... of the field (Matt. 6:30).

4. Jesus said that fulfilled prophecy is to help us to .... (John 13:19).
5. We are made partakers of the divine nature by the precious .... (2 Peter 1:4).
6. We are .... through the words our Lord has spoken (John 15:3).
7. God's promises are .... and .... (2 Cor. 1:20).

Correct Answers
1. God
2. wisdom
3. grass
4. believe

5. promises
6. clean
7. yea, Amen

Assignment

As our distress was great in connection with our problem referred to in this lesson, so it may be great with others in relation to *their* specific problems. We suggest that you review this lesson several times. As you do, articulate your faith. Do not speak your doubts, if such you have. Claim the presence of the Holy Spirit, who "helpeth our infirmities" (Rom. 8:26). He will help us to speak even the *little* faith we have rather than the large doubts Satan tempts us with. Then may be fulfilled the promise: "With the mouth confession is made unto salvation" (chap. 10:10).

Lesson Guide

8

SATISFYING FELLOWSHIP
Fulfilling Man's Social Needs

In our ministry we have discovered that one of the relatively untapped sources of strength in many Christian lives is that of social fellowship in Christ. We do not refer to fellowship in entertainment, but to prayer fellowship. To many, the word *prayer* does not represent fellowship, but in the Christian life, it is satisfying indeed. This prayer fellowship will be for other souls, for the needs of our brothers and sisters in Christ, and for our own needs.

1. The Joy of Finding the Lost. "What man of you, having an hundred sheep, if he lose one of them, doth not leave the ninety and nine in the wilderness, and go after that which is lost, until he find it? And when he hath found it, he layeth it on his shoulders, rejoicing" (Luke 15:4, 5).

2. This Social Fellowship May Be of a Few or of Many. "For where two or three are gathered together in my name, there am I in the midst of them" (Matt. 18:20).

Jesus took with Him "Peter, James, and John" (chap. 17:1). "And when the day of Pentecost was fully come, they were all with one accord in one place" (Acts 2:1).

3. In This Fellowship We May Become the Answer to the Craving of Others for Christian Sympathy. Many church members would be happy to share Christian fellowship in prayer circles, but they do not know how to begin. We hope that the experience we describe here will bless you as you decide to let our Lord help you find a prayer partner.

We decided to experiment in a city where we did not know the members of the church. We visited home after home, encouraging each man to meet with another man once a week for an hour, studying our lessons and applying them. Sisters in the church were encouraged to do the same.

4. Claiming the Promise for the Holy Spirit and Wisdom. Before each visit we claimed the promises of Luke 11:13 and James 1:5. The Holy Spirit gave us the wisdom we needed in making appointments by telephone with those we planned to visit. As we talked in the homes, we looked for any need the people had that we could fulfill, claiming God's promises to help them. When they began visiting, they, too, would claim the same promises of our Lord. They would pray and study how to meet their friends at points of specific need, even as we had theirs.

5. Prayers for Help Answered. At the very first home we visited, the brother was thrilled. He told us he was sure that God sent us to him at that particular hour; not more than five minutes before we telephoned, he was in the bathroom spitting up blood. He was frightened and prayed most earnestly, "Dear Lord, please send someone to help me." We prayed for his healing. We also explained to him the joys of prayer partnerships. He immediately responded. Before the week was over, he had found his prayer partner. Also, the indications were that he was healed of his ailment.

6. The Futility of Pressure. "Not by might, nor by

power, but by my spirit, saith the Lord of hosts" (Zech. 4:6).

Claiming the promise of the Holy Spirit, and asking for wisdom, we visited another home. The woman shared with us a story of a near tragedy. Months before, she had pressured her husband into going to the altar during a call in a revival series. He was sitting there as she told the sad story of how he did not want to create a dispute and so was baptized. But he was not converted. In the days and weeks that followed the baptism, she nagged him about his conduct until he returned to drink. We sat there as good listeners, prayerfully asking our Lord to help us not to criticize her for her mistakes. We expressed our sympathy for both of them and gave her hope.

When we talked to her about prayer partnerships, she was immediately pleased. She stated she knew a woman who, she felt sure, would want to meet with her for an hour a week.

7. *Instead of Demanding, We Allure.* As we visited home after home, the people saw that we wanted to contribute to their happiness. One woman stated she was on the verge of losing her husband. She told us it was because she had demanded that he spend more time at home. The result was that he spent far less time with her. She determined to begin a prayer-partnership program. She would learn not only the science of prayer but also the science of communication so that she would not make demands on others' love. Instead, she would aid them in their need. Instead of repelling them, she would draw them by Christ's love.

In one church we served, 150 prayer partnerships were begun in ten days. Many miracles were reported by the leaders of that church.

Study Guide 8

Quiz

1. When the Good Shepherd finds His wandering sheep, He brings it home with .... (Luke 15:4, 5).
2. What does our Lord promise us in Luke 11:13? ....
3. In James 1:5 God promises us ....
4. What did Jesus miraculously produce at the marriage feast in Cana of Galilee? .... (John 2:1-11).
5. We love our Lord because He first .... (1 John 4:19).
6. True or false: A part of the message of the book of Genesis is that God is endeavoring to get through to us. ....

Correct Answers

1. rejoicing
2. the Holy Spirit
3. wisdom
4. wine
5. loved us
6. true

Assignment

If you have not yet found a prayer partner, try to find one this week. If you hesitate because of timidity, or if one you ask to join you gives excuses, request your pastor to help you find one. I have at times made public calls for those who would like to be prayer partners. Then we have matched names, and prayer-partner programs have been started.

Lesson Guide

9

"BEGONE, LEGALISM!"
Conditions to Answered Prayer Are Promised Gifts

When we began to learn the science of the prayer of faith years ago—the Prayer of Reception (Matt. 21:22)—we were thrilled. We were eager to share it; others, we determined, must learn this beautiful science.

But there were those conditions to prayer that many considered difficult, conditions that bothered many professed Christians. How could we present them the way God wanted us to? We asked for wisdom, and believed He was giving it. We returned thanks that He had given us wisdom to show conditions in the proper light. And then light came. We were delighted.

Here was the answer: God does not demand of man anything that he cannot do with His help. God never expects man to do it alone. Could man fulfill the conditions without God, he would not need to pray.

In other words, the very conditions guarantee that they can be fulfilled, because God provides the answer with the condition. Some answers are given to us long before we ask. Others come with our asking, believing, and claiming. But every condition to prayer brings a free gift. A few examples of the conditions are:

1. Faith Is Both a Condition and a Free Gift. "But without faith it is impossible to please him" (Heb. 11:6). "God hath dealt to every man the measure of faith" (Rom. 12:3).

We do not need to lament our lack of faith. God has already dealt faith to everyone who accepts Jesus. All we need to do is exercise it, and it will grow.

"But the fruit of the Spirit is . . . faith" (Gal. 5:22). If we want more faith, we continue to ask, believe, and claim His Holy Spirit, and to exercise faith. The fruit will grow. Faith is a free gift—absolutely without price. It came by no effort of ours. But the need to exercise it is ours. (See lesson 13 on ways by which faith is strengthened.)

2. Repentance for Sin Is Both a Condition and a Promised Gift. "If I regard iniquity in my heart, the Lord will not hear me" (Ps. 66:18).

"Him [Jesus] hath God exalted with his right hand to . . . give repentance" (Acts 5:31).

God's everlasting love is continually offering repentance as a free gift to the one who will ask, believe, and receive it. God says of us as He did of Judah, "With lovingkindness have I drawn thee" (Jer. 31:3). It is, therefore, up to each one of us to reach up and take the proffered gift of repentance for sin. We can give up sin only as we accept the deliverance God offers us as a gift.

We became acquainted with a fine young married couple whose deep sincerity impressed us greatly. Their winsomeness won our hearts; their Christlike simplicity delighted us. One year later we met them again in another city. The wife, as precious to us as ever, had become infatuated with a man half her age. But she was trapped. She was a slave. She cherished this sinful infatuation and would not let go.

We could have said to her, "If you will let go of this cherished sin, we will ask God to help you." But she was a prisoner in the cell of the evil one. She did not know how to unlock the door.

Someone else had to bring her freedom. Someone

else had to bring her a hatred for the sin she cherished, and *Someone* has promised to do this. His name is Jesus Christ. "If the Son therefore shall make you free, ye shall be free indeed" (John 8:36). The Holy Spirit inspired the prophet of old to prophesy of Jesus that He would "proclaim liberty to the captives" (Isa. 61:1). He would "put enmity" in the heart for Satan and all that he stands for (Gen. 3:15).

For us to tell this woman to give up her cherished sin would have been to mock her. She was so frustrated that she did not even have reasoning powers to exercise her faith. So we exercised faith for her. We claimed the promise of Matthew 18:19: "If two of you shall agree on earth as touching any thing that they shall ask, it shall be done for them of my Father which is in heaven."

After we had counseled with her, we had suggested that we pray about the problem. But as we started to kneel, she repeated again and again in her frustration, "I do not have the faith that God will deliver me." Again and again we enthusiastically responded, "Rest on our faith. We believe. Jesus promised that the faith of two of us will do it." We opened the Bible to Hebrews 2:14, 15, and read how He will deliver them who "were all their lifetime subject to bondage." Since God can deliver lifetime bondmen, surely He can deliver those who have been bound only a few months. There was no question about it.

We told her of the two geese who flapped their wings in midair under a wounded goose and carried it along. We told her we were doing something similar for her.

God fulfilled His promise and set her free from the cherished sin. The next day she testified of the remarkable deliverance.

That woman was delighted that God had freed her from bondage. She was thrilled that He had put enmity in her heart for the thing she was clinging to—that He had set her free. She and her husband became beautiful workers for Jesus Christ.

Not all sinners are as helpless as this woman was in the exercise of faith. Thousands can reach up and take the proffered gift of repentance while they sit under the shade of an oak tree, or in a church pew, or beside a rippling brook.

3. Obedience Is a Condition, But the Heart to Obey Is Also a Free Gift. "And whatsoever we ask, we receive of him, because we keep his commandments, and do those things that are pleasing in his sight" (1 John 3:22). "I will . . . cause you to walk in my statutes" (Eze. 36:27). "I will put my laws into their mind" (Heb. 8:10).

We had the privilege of baptizing two young men who had spent years in the drug world, smoking, drinking, running the route of sex, LSD, marijuana, and so on. Then they began reading the gospel story. In four days one found eternal life. The other found it in about ten days.

Years before, one of the young men had tried the route of obedience as a condition that he supposed he was to fulfill on his own. But he seemed unable to get help to obey from God. He did not know that God promises the power for obedience as a free gift. The obedience that God requires is not something that one can do on his own power. Rather, it is something God gives the sinner the power to do. On the basis of this gift, the sinner dares to ask for more and still more blessings, all unmerited.

Over the years since their conversion experience, these young men have been used by the Holy Spirit to lead thousands to express an assurance of eternal life through what they call an "assurance session." This session is based on free gifts that come from the bountiful hand of the One who was crucified on Calvary.

One of the promises these men lead their hearers in claiming is Ezekiel 36:26, 27: "A new heart also will I give you. . . . And ye shall keep my judgments, and do them."

4. Diligence and Perseverance Are Both Conditions and Free Gifts. "I will strengthen thee" (Isa. 41:10).

We believe that God will do for human ministers what He does for His angel ministers. "[God] who maketh . . . his ministers a flame of fire" (Heb. 1:7). We have claimed this free gift repeatedly. Can you imagine a minister asking, believing, and claiming this promise, and then preaching a sleepy sermon? Can you visualize a soul winner claiming this promise and telling silly jokes?

A reminder:

Remember that witnessing, or confessing Christ, involves not merely our talk but also our lives (2 Cor. 3:1-3). Confessing Christ is not primarily giving Bible studies on doctrinal topics. It is talking about Him, witnessing to His love, His mercy, His grace, how He keeps His promises to all who acknowledge their unworthiness and believe in Him.

Unselfish sharing is one of the big conditions to answered prayer. Read the story of the man who asked his friend for three loaves that he might share (Luke 11:2-13). This is the setting of Christ's ABC's of prayer.

We thank Thee, Lord, that "every good gift and every perfect gift is from above" (James 1:17).

A Personal Message

We are frequently tempted to tell another individual what he must do to receive the favor of God before he really knows God. This can be a grave mistake. It is important to remember that the other person may be a *slave* to sin. He may be like a *prisoner* in a cell and you are telling him to do certain things he can only do *outside* his cell. To suggest such is but to mock his frustration.

What a prisoner needs is to have the doors opened. There is an open door to freedom. That door is Jesus Christ, His love and His power. He promises, "If the Son therefore shall make you free, ye shall be free indeed" (John 8:36).

If a man could get rid of the guilt of his sins by himself, he would not need a Saviour. If a man could obey in his own strength, he would not need the Holy Spirit. If he could fulfill the conditions of prayer by himself, he would not need God's gifts.

Thus, in our efforts to help others, we must do all we can to point them to Christ, the open Door, the Door to freedom. We need to act like Jesus. We need to have an unshockable attitude toward the fallen. No matter what another does, we are to love him just the same, fellowship with him just the same, as we would want one in Christ to fellowship with us if we had fallen.

We need to share the good news that repentance for sin is a gift, that forgiveness is a gift, that cleansing from sin is a gift, that strength for obedience is a gift. As we have reached up and *asked, believed,* and *claimed* these free gifts as promised by our Lord, so we are to help and encourage others to do the same.

Quiz

1. Has God already given every Christian faith? Yes............ No............ (Rom. 12:3).
2. We do not work ourselves up to get repentance, for it is a .... gift (Acts 5:31).
3. God is eager to deliver people who all their lifetime were subject to .... (Heb. 2:14, 15).
4. God promises to put His laws in our .... (Heb. 8:10).

Correct Answers

1. yes
2. free

3. bondage
4. minds

Assignment

In a prayer partnership or group, discuss the first three conditions for answered prayer, *faith, repentance,* and *obedience.* Then spend a few moments emphasizing the importance of perseverance. Many believers have a tendency to give up praying for a particular matter if the answer does not come as quickly as anticipated.

Lesson Guide

10 ✳

ANSWERS DELAYED? WHY?
Conditions of Humility

There are at least seven aspects of humility that are conditions to answered prayer.

1. *Humility Feels Its Need.* "Blessed are they which do hunger and thirst after righteousness: for they shall be filled" (Matt. 5:6). "I will pour water upon him that is thirsty, and floods upon the dry ground" (Isa. 44:3). "He hath filled the hungry with good things; and the rich he hath sent empty away" (Luke 1:53).

Not long after my wife and I began to discover the science of prayer, we had an unforgettable experience. With some close friends, who were themselves seeking to learn the science of prayer, we attended divine worship one Sabbath. Our custom is to seek earnestly God's Holy Spirit as we approach the presence of the Lord, and to ask Him to feed our hungry souls.

Although the speaker of the morning was not the most interesting, we received four distinct blessings during his sermon. But when we left the sanctuary, a young friend began to criticize the service, the speaker, and the sermon.

We listened for a while in silence and then ventured to ask him a question. "When you entered the sanctuary this morning, did you ask God to feed your hungry soul?" A puzzled expression was on his face as he replied, "Why, no." But in another instant he understood the meaning of the question. We explained to him, "This is why you did not receive a blessing. We received four specific blessings today because we felt our need."

2. Humility Leaves the "How" and "When" to God.
"And I will bring the blind by a way that they knew not; I will lead them in paths that they have not known" (Isa. 42:16).

"Call unto me, and I will answer thee, and shew thee great and mighty things, which thou knowest not" (Jer. 33:3).

Let God answer your prayers in His way.

There was a couple who asked God to fulfill the promise of Philippians 4:19, which says, "My God shall supply all your need according to his riches in glory by Christ Jesus." This text definitely promises to fulfill our need. We have a right through Christ to ask that our need be met.

But this conscientious couple not only asked that their need be met, they also specified *how* that need must be met. They not only prayed for a house (which was their need) but also told God *which* house to give them, its location, and all.

The promise does not say, "I will give you a house on the very street *you* specify." It does not say, "I will give you a house on the very road you name." It only promises to supply our need. If we need a house, trust in God will let Him decide which house will fill our need. We may find a house on Main Street. We may also discover there is a house out on Roseberry Lane.

We have a perfect right, we emphasize, to ask God to supply our need. But since "your Father knoweth what things ye have need of, before ye ask him" (Matt. 6:8), we are to let Him make the choice for us.

When the couple learned that they had gone too far in their prayer request, they repented. They humbly told God they would let *Him* choose which house they needed. Immediately God gave them the very house *they* thought was best.

Another illustration of this condition to answered prayer is that of claiming a promise for the salvation of some soul. In 1 John 5:16 God definitely promises life to the child of God who has lost his way, if we pray believingly and fulfill the conditions. But a young man who decided that the very soul for whom he prayed *must* be converted that very day went beyond the promise.

There is no Bible promise that a person will accept Christ the very day we choose. God knows the heart of the one for whom we pray. God knows how to weave influences around a life that will result in an individual choosing the victory He offers. It may take longer than we would choose. We would do much better not to ask God to answer our prayer on the day *we* decide.

Repeatedly, saints of God come to us excitedly telling us they have asked, believed, and thanked Him that a certain person would be at a specific meeting. They think that because they have prayed they have every assurance this loved one will be present at that very hour. They are tremendously disappointed if it does not take place. They have overlooked the fact that there is no promise in the Bible that people will attend a specific church service at the specific hour we choose.

We emphasize—we have every right to claim salvation for any tempted and tried member of the body of Christ. But when we ask for something that the Lord has never promised, we must change our prayer. It should then be, not a prayer of reception, but one of commitment. It should then go something like this: "Dear Lord, You have promised me in 1 John 5:16 that You will save John Doe. I ask believingly. I claim triumphantly. I thank You I have received. Now, dear Lord, *if it be Your will* according to the circumstances and the heart of John Doe, may he also attend the meeting to be held in the church at 3:30 P.M. today. In Jesus' name. Amen."

The part that claims the promise is a prayer of reception. The part that exceeds what the promise offers must be a prayer of request.

In this connection another fact is essential, having to do with God's priorities. God has promised us eternal life (1 John 2:25). We have a right to ask, believe, and thank Him that we have received eternal life, having met the conditions. But if we ask for patience, God promises that the way patience can be developed is through suffering, trials, and tribulations (see Isa. 48:10; James 1:2, 3; Rev. 14:12).

For the surrendered Christian to claim eternal life is within the area of prayer of reception. But to pray for eternal life with no suffering, no problems, or no trials in the present life is wrong. It ignores the necessity of experiences that help to develop firmness of character, patience, and longsuffering. So to pray that we will have no trials is to pray contrary to the Word of God.

However, we have a right to pray for strength to bear these trials—for grace to overcome them. This is in accordance with the Word of God. We may ask. We may believe. We may thank God we have received that strength. This is part of the science of prayer (see Jude 24; Phil. 4:13; 1 Cor. 10:13).

 3. Humility Asks for the Gift of a Forgiving Spirit. A forgiving spirit is a condition to answered prayer. "What things soever ye desire, when ye pray, believe that ye receive them, and ye shall have them. And when ye stand praying, forgive, if ye have ought against any: that your Father also which is in heaven may forgive you your trespasses" (Mark 11:24, 25).

A new heart, from which a forgiving spirit springs, is also a promised gift.

"A new heart also will I give you, and a new spirit will I put within you: and I will take away the stony heart out of your flesh, and I will give you an heart of flesh" (Eze. 36:26).

It is important to learn just how God gives us this new spirit.

"I will put my spirit within you, and cause you to walk in my statutes" (verse 27).

The Holy Spirit makes clear on what basis He will give us this new attitude—the spirit of forgiveness.

"We . . . beholding . . . are changed into the same image . . . by the Spirit of the Lord" (2 Cor. 3:18).

Following the principle carefully, for example, we cease to think about what unfair advantage a person took of us, and fix the mind on what Jesus did for us on Calvary. Putting it another way: Instead of thinking of how we do not deserve what that person did to us, we will think of how we do not deserve what Jesus did for us on the hill called Golgotha.

Many years ago I was involved in a great trouble. I went alone in the woods and brooded in self-pity, thinking of the injustice a few people had heaped on me. The more I brooded over what they had done, the weaker I became, and the less forgiving I felt. Then the Holy Spirit flashed this text into my mind: "Consider him that endured such contradiction of sinners against himself, lest ye be wearied and faint in your minds" (Heb. 12:3).

Foggily, I began to think of Jesus before Pilate and Herod. My eyes were so overcast with clouds of self-pity I could scarcely see Jesus even in my imagination. But I forced myself to do what the scripture commanded. And as, in my mind, the outline of our dear Lord became clearer and clearer, the bitterness vanished. Forgiveness took its place.

Let us never forget that while the spirit that forgives our enemies is a condition for answered prayer, it is also a free gift. It is ours if we will take our eyes off the problem and place them on the solution—the love of

Christ for us, who are so unworthy.)

A sister in the church was very ill with an abdominal tumor. Before she realized the seriousness of her malady, the tumor had grown so large that her doctor told her he could not do surgery until she regained some of her strength. But try as she might, it proved impossible. In her agony she sent an urgent request for a minister, a great man of God, to come and pray for her healing. When he arrived, he asked her in deep seriousness about her relationship to God. She replied that it was good. Then he asked about her relationship with people. She replied that all was well except for one thing. She went on to tell about a flood that had inundated the home of a friend of hers. Our sister had opened her own guest home to this unfortunate flood victim. She explained to her guest that there would be no rent, just the electric bill. But when her guest left for her own home she did not have the courtesy to so much as pay the electric bill. "And that wasn't right."

Then, to her astonishment, the pastor opened his briefcase, put the Bible in it, closed the briefcase, and turned to leave. As he was walking out of the room he said gravely, "When you have straightened out your problem of unforgiveness, call me."

For three full days our sister went through great agony of mind. Then she was willing for the Holy Spirit to give her a forgiving spirit, and peace came to her troubled breast.

When the pastor returned at her next urgent plea, he asked the same questions. Was everything all right between her and the Lord, and between her and others? She exclaimed with assurance that everything was all right. The pastor suggested to her that she take a little more time examining her heart while he went out for a short walk. When he returned she exclaimed joyfully that she knew all was well. God had given her a new attitude, a new heart of humble forgiveness for that thoughtless woman.

As the minister prayed for her and anointed her, our sister later explained that she felt as though a knife were cutting around the tumor, yet without pain. She knew she had been healed, and began praising the Lord with tears of joy. She felt her abdomen contract to its original size.

When her husband returned home that evening, he was astonished at the appearance of his wife. "Ethel," he asked, "what has happened?"

"Honey, Jesus has been here and I have been healed!"

Friends, sometimes our Lord delays answers to our prayers until we accept from His great heart of love forgiveness for all who have hurt us.

4. Humility Seeks Answers We Can Share With Others.

It is not selfish to pray, "Give us this day our daily bread" (Matt. 6:11). It is not selfish to ask for our needs. "My God shall supply all your need" (Phil. 4:19). God is exceedingly willing to give extra blessings when we ask in order to share with others.

"Friend, lend me three loaves; for a friend of mine in his journey is come to me, and I have nothing to set before him. . . . I say unto you, Ask, and it shall be given you; seek, and ye shall find; knock, and it shall be opened unto you" (Luke 11:5-9).

He who seeks answers for selfish reasons cannot really expect answers to his prayer. "Ye ask, and receive not, because ye ask amiss, that ye may consume it upon your lusts" (James 4:3).

In our ministry we have repeatedly received rich rewards when sharing unselfishly with others. Pages could be written describing these tremendous blessings. When we have asked that we might share the cup of blessing with others, God caused it to overflow. We were showered with Heaven's favors.

5. *Humility Does Not Have a Holier-than-thou Attitude.* A holier-than-thou attitude is a smoke in our Lord's nostrils: "I have spread out my hands all the day unto a rebellious people . . . which say, Stand by thyself, come not near to me; for I am holier than thou. . . . These are a smoke in my nose" (Isa. 65:2-5).

Those who are continually finding in others things that in their judgment are sin cannot expect God to accept their prayers. In all prayer groups we steer away from criticism of others.

6. *Humility Prays in the Name and Merits of Jesus Christ.* "Whatsoever ye shall ask of the Father in my name, he may give it you" (John 15:16).

Christ assures us that when we are truly His children and then ask according to His will and in His name, our requests will be granted.

7. *Humility Does Not Take Credit That Belongs to God.* "And call upon me in the day of trouble: I will deliver thee, and thou shalt glorify me" (Ps. 50:15).

Did you ever think of just plain honesty as being an aspect of humility? It can be illustrated this way: A man is in trouble. Helpless, he cannot find a way out. Then he asks God to come to his rescue and God does.

Later, friends come along and praise the man for the wonderful wisdom he showed in difficult circumstances. The man accepts this flattery. He never tells them that he did not have the wisdom, he did not have the answers, that in utter helplessness he sought God, and that the entire solution came from God.

His lack of humility was plain dishonesty. He did not deserve the credit his friends heaped upon him. He yielded to their flattery. He knew it was only God's love, power, and wisdom that saved the day. But he wanted his friends to think that it came from himself.

When men take credit for what they did not accomplish, it is dishonesty. Pride is dishonesty. Humility is honesty. It is merely telling others the truth of the matter. Humility says, "I was in trouble. I was helpless. I knew no way out. I prayed and God answered. I deserve no credit whatsoever. It all belongs to God."

Can you imagine people then turning to him and exclaiming, "You are so very humble!" If such were the case he should reply, "No, I am just being honest. I have told you exactly as it is. It was God alone who did the deed. He alone gave the solution."

Study Guide 10

A Personal Message

The previous lesson has to do with humility. We learned there that we must allow the Holy Spirit to give us humility. And in our work for others, we must add to this a factor we discussed in another lesson, freedom of choice for the other person. These two factors—*humility* and *choice*—are important aspects of the quality *human ease.*

We should graciously give another person perfect freedom, without trying to pressure him, to preach at him, or nag him. This observes the law of *choice.* We obey the law of *humility* by not belittling another. This adds to the individual's feeling of security in our presence.

Jesus said, in effect, If you choose to come to Me, all you who are weary and heavy laden—if you choose to accept of My humility—you will find rest to your souls. You will be at ease (see Matt. 11:28-30).

If we speak one remark belittling another, we are breaking the law of humility. If we try to tell him what to do without his wanting to know, we break the law of choice. When we do one or both of these, he is likely to lose interest in our witness. Let us examine ourselves. Does any individual we contact say, in effect, "You may come to see me, but leave your religion at home"? If so, we should discover whether we are perhaps forgetting the two secrets *choice* and *humility.*

If we cannot try to urge our convictions on others,

how can they be convicted of their sins and turn to the Lord? The Holy Spirit is promised as a Reprover of sin (John 16:8). If we do not nag or belittle other people, the Holy Spirit's voice can get through to them. Then they will be more likely to recognize the conviction as divine and to surrender to the Lord. Our part is to be a witness, not a judge.

Quiz

1. If we would find answers to our prayers, we must .... and thirst after righteousness (Matt. 5:6).
2. God often answers in a way we know .... (Jer. 33:3).
3. Can we expect wonderful answers to our prayers if we refuse to forgive others? ....
4. "Ye ask, and receive not, because ye ask amiss, that ye may consume it upon your ...." (James 4:3).
5. A people with a holier-than-thou attitude are .... in God's nose (Isa. 65:3, 5).
6. We are to ask in the name and merits of .... (John 15:16).
7. When God answers our prayers, are we to give self, or God, the credit? ....

Correct Answers

1. hunger
2. not
3. no
4. lusts
5. smoke
6. Jesus
7. God

11

"JESUS DISOBEYED ME!"
How to Avoid Presumptive Prayers

As we saw in study seven, two of my brothers were gravely concerned for us in a very difficult experience we had. They frankly expressed the opinion that we were guilty of presumption in prayer. But they had never really studied the meaning of the word *presumption.*

The psalmist cried to God: "Keep back thy servant also from presumptuous sins; let them not have dominion over me: then shall I be upright, and I shall be innocent from the great transgression" (Ps. 19:13).

In *Young's Analytical Concordance to the Holy Scripture* we are told that the meaning of the word *presumptuous,* as used in Psalm 19:13, is "to act proudly." Therefore, in his prayer the psalmist was saying, "Dear Lord, keep me from having a proud attitude in prayer. Then I will be upright, and I will be innocent of the great transgression."

To keep from acting proudly in prayer, we should observe the following:

1. *Instead of Presuming to Tell God How to Answer Our Prayers, We Should Completely Surrender Our Plans to His Infinite Judgment.* Here is an example of presumptuous prayer. A little girl, whom we shall call Mary, was moving with her parents from one city to another about 1,000 miles away. Mary had a pet dog named Troubles, but her parents decided it was better not to take Troubles with them to the next city. But Mary was rebellious. So to secure what her little heart wanted, she began to pray. But she did not ask God to work it out *His* way. She said, "Dear Jesus, when we arrive at the new city, have Troubles there." But there is no promise in the Bible that a dog will go by some magic UFO transport to a distant city even though a little girl does love its companionship. God does promise to supply our need (Phil. 4:19). But Mary had "need of patience" (Heb. 10:36) to develop her character.

When Mary began school in the new city, she became acquainted with another girl about her age to whom she unburdened her heart, her rebellion, and her self-will. "I have prayed to Jesus. I told Him to have Troubles here when we arrived." Then she concluded by saying, "But Jesus disobeyed me."

Job was an example of one who kept away from a presumptuous prayer. In the midst of great frustration, including the misunderstanding of close friends, he revealed the opposite of a presumptuous spirit: "Though he slay me, yet will I trust in him," he said (Job 13:15).

2. Do Not Claim That an Answered Prayer Is Proof That We Are Right if We Are in Deliberate Transgression. We need to submit to God's sanctification. God's mercy is not extended merely to righteous people. "For he maketh his sun to rise on the evil and on the good" (Matt. 5:45).

God gave Judas power "against unclean spirits, to cast them out, and heal all manner of sickness and all manner of disease" (chap. 10:1-4).

"Many will say to me in that day, Lord, Lord, have we not prophesied in thy name? and in thy name have cast out devils? and in thy name done many wonderful works? And then will I profess unto them, I never knew you: depart from me, ye that work iniquity" (chap. 7: 22, 23).

We should avoid praying a prayer that ignores conditions or that asks God to overlook transgressions. Satan, quoting a promise in the Bible, tempted our Lord to cast Himself down from the Temple. But he cleverly omitted the part of the promise that shows it was conditioned upon our following God's ways (chap. 4:6). Jesus rejected this temptation with a firm statement of Scripture (verse 7).

To expect God to answer our prayers when we presumptuously transgress is a sin we must avoid.

3. Avoid the Prayer That Expects God to Compromise So That We Can Hold the World in One Hand and the Hand of Jesus in the Other.

"Love not the world, neither the things that are in the world. If any man love the world, the love of the Father is not in him. For all that is in the world, the lust of the flesh, and the lust of the eyes, and the pride of life, is not of the Father, but is of the world" (1 John 2:15, 16).

To avoid praying presumptuously, we read the experience of the psalmist, who cried out, "I have set the Lord always before me: because he is at my right hand, I shall not be moved" (Ps. 16:8).

4. Avoid Asking God to Heal Us Physically Without Asking Him to Heal Us Spiritually Also.

"Ye ask, and receive not, because ye ask amiss, that ye may consume it upon your lusts" (James 4:3).

"Afterward Jesus findeth him in the temple, and said unto him, Behold, thou art made whole: sin no more, lest a worse thing come unto thee" (John 5:14).

A person requesting physical healing should earnestly ask himself the question, Do I expect God to heal me so that I may uplift self or so that I may indulge in activities God condemns? To expect God to heal under such circumstances is presumption. "Beloved, I wish above all things that thou mayest prosper and be in health, even as thy soul prospereth" (3 John 2).

Physical affliction was a big part of the bitter Gethsemane I previously referred to. As we asked God to heal my body, I added in my heart: "Dear God, I am not asking You to heal my body so that my soul may be lost. But rather I ask You to heal my *soul* with my body. I do not ask Thee, dear Lord, to heal my body and then let me forget Thee and lose eternal life. Therefore, dear Lord, I request the physical healing to blend with the spiritual restoration."

In my early ministry I had learned a sad lesson. I asked only for physical healing for a man who had suffered a stroke. He was miraculously healed through prayer, but his first journey after healing was to a woman with whom he had been living in sin.

Let us pray to God to forgive all our iniquity as well as to heal all our diseases (Ps. 103:3).

5. When We Pray for Victory Over Sin, We Should Ask God to Give Us Strength to Keep Away From Temptation. "Abstain from all appearance of evil" (1 Thess. 5:22). "Lead us not into temptation" (Matt. 6:13).

"Enter not into the path of the wicked, and go not in the way of evil men. Avoid it, pass not by it, turn from it, and pass away." "Let thine eyes look right on, and let thine eyelids look straight before thee. . . . Turn not to the right hand nor to the left: remove thy foot from evil" (Prov. 4:14, 15, 25-27).

A minister preached a sermon entitled "The Second Look," in which he pointed out that "evil" walks down our streets almost in the nude. We see it in our newspapers, magazines, on the television, and we hear it on the radio. He stated that the first unintentional look, which we cannot avoid, does not defile the soul. But defilement comes when we take a second look, knowing that we have opened the chambers of the soul to evil, to lust, to sin. Let the prayer of the psalmist be ours: "Keep back thy servant also from presumptuous sins; let them not have dominion over me: then shall I be upright, and I shall be innocent from the great transgression" (Ps. 19:13).

6. Presumption Often Has a Holier-than-thou Attitude. "I have spread out my hands all the day unto a rebellious people . . . which say, Stand by thyself, come not near to me; for I am holier than thou. These are smoke in my nose, a fire that burneth all the day" (Isa. 65:5).

God tells how we may avoid this presumption. It is to "take away from . . . thee . . . the putting forth of the finger, and speaking vanity" (chap. 58:9).

Imagine a person putting forth his finger as he points to what he judges as unworthy motive in another. It has often been observed that when we point at another, we are actually pointing three fingers—the three folded fingers—at ourselves. When we judge others, we point a finger of condemnation at ourselves: "For wherein thou judgest another, thou condemnest thyself; for thou that judgest doest the same things" (Rom. 2:1).

7. Though We May Have Been Guilty of Presumptuous Sin, if We Repent, God Promises Wonderful Answers. "Then shalt thou call, and the Lord shall answer; thou shalt cry, and he shall say, Here I am. If thou take away from the midst of thee the yoke, the putting forth of the finger, and speaking vanity; . . . and the Lord shall guide thee continually, and satisfy thy soul in drought, and make fat thy bones: and thou shalt be like a watered garden, and like a spring of water, whose waters fail not" (Isa. 58:9-11).

A Personal Message

A holier-than-thou attitude has no part in true soul winning. To be shocked when John Doe tells us of some of his sins is to create a gap between him and us. Many professed Christians think a shocked appearance is the way to bring John to conviction. But this is a false concept of conviction.

Jesus made clear that conviction of sin comes from the Holy Spirit (John 16:8). Our work is to uplift Jesus. Our part is to witness to what He has done for our unworthy lives. And let us not forget that word—*unworthy.*

To admit that we are unworthy does not mean we are to relate sordid sins of which we may have been guilty. It simply means that we recognize we have no merits of our own and have done nothing to deserve reward. Having made the admission, we are in a position to witness to the power of Jesus Christ.

Assuming an unshocked attitude at the knowledge of John Doe's sins, without giving the slightest impression that sin is not sin, is an art. This is one reason why we should claim the promise of the Holy Spirit (Luke 11:13) as we visit John. And this is why we should claim the promise for wisdom (James 1:5).

It may take much prayer on our part to be kept from exhorting the one we are trying to win, to be kept from preaching at him, to be kept from *telling* him. Instead of trying to instruct the person who has not asked for instruction, we are to express confidence in him, hope for him, and show him selfless love.

Quiz

1. When we begin making demands of God, we should remember we have need of .... (Heb. 10:36).
2. To many people who claim to have wrought many miracles Jesus will say, "I .... knew you" (Matt. 7:23).
3. Can we hold on to the sensuous pleasures of the world and Jesus at the same time? .... (1 John 2:15, 16).
4. Jesus told a healed man to .... no more (John 5:14).
5. We should abstain from .... appearance of evil (1 Thess. 5:22).
6. When we point the finger of judgment at others, how many do we point at ourselves? ....
7. If we stop judging and condemning others and are unselfish, God will guide us .... (Isa. 59:9-11).

Correct Answers
1. patience
2. never
3. no
4. sin

5. all
6. three
7. continually

Assignment

When your Prayer-Fellowship group has grown to six or seven individuals, you may consider dividing into two groups. Thus each group can keep growing and dividing until a large segment of the church is involved.

Lesson Guide **12**

CONVERTED AGAINST HER WILL?
Why I Love the Holy Spirit

We do not give the Lord deadlines in conversion of a soul. Probably we have not asked God to meet deadlines more than five times in our entire ministry of more than five decades. But in the experience we now relate, the Holy Spirit strongly impressed us one day that He would do a thorough work for Maria that very week. Since we are promised that He will guide us (Ps. 32:8), we reached out in faith and claimed Maria's commitment to God.

During that week we left all the conviction to the Holy Spirit (John 16:8).

1. The Holy Spirit Makes Entirely Unnecessary a Do-it-yourself Program of Works. "This is the word of the Lord unto Zerubbabel, saying, Not by might, nor by power, but by my spirit, saith the Lord of hosts. Who art thou, O great mountain? before Zerubbabel thou shalt become a plain: and he shall bring forth the headstone thereof with shoutings, crying, Grace, grace unto it" (Zech. 4:6, 7).

2. The Holy Spirit Brings the New Birth; We Must Not Try to Work Ourselves Into a Frenzy to Be Born Again. "But as many as received him, to them gave he power to become the sons of God, even to them that believe on his name: which were born, not of blood, nor of the will of the flesh, nor of the will of man, but of

God" (John 1:12, 13). "Jesus answered, Verily, verily, I say unto thee, Except a man be born of water and of the Spirit, he cannot enter into the kingdom of God. That which is born of the flesh is flesh; and that which is born of the Spirit is spirit. Marvel not that I said unto thee, Ye must be born again" (chap. 3:5-7).

3. We Do Not Lay Our Own Plans. God Lays the Plans and We Accept Them. "In all thy ways acknowledge him, and he shall direct thy paths" (Prov. 3:6).

4. The Holy Spirit Makes Us Christ-centered. He Keeps Us From Focusing on Self and Selfish Problems. "But when the Comforter is come, whom I will send unto you from the Father, even the Spirit of truth, which proceedeth from the Father, he shall testify of me" (John 15:26).

"But we all, with open face beholding as in a glass the glory of the Lord, are changed into the same image from glory to glory, even as by the Spirit of the Lord" (2 Cor. 3:18).

5. The Spirit Gives the Ability to Present Jesus to the Sinner Instead of Focusing His Mind on Matters Diverting From Christ. "But ye shall receive power, after that the Holy Ghost is come upon you: and ye shall be witnesses unto *me* both in Jerusalem, and in all Judea, and in Samaria, and unto the uttermost part of the earth" (Acts 1:8).

Peter's Spirit-filled, Pentecostal sermon uplifted Jesus in a mighty way.

6. The Holy Spirit Brings a Joy to the Newborn Believer That Continues as Long as the Spirit Leads. "Create in me a clean heart, O God; and renew a right spirit within me. . . . Restore unto me the joy of thy salvation; and uphold me with thy free spirit. Then will

I teach transgressors thy ways; and sinners shall be converted unto thee" (Ps. 51:10-13).

"Now when they heard this, they were pricked in their heart, and said unto Peter and to the rest of the apostles, Men and brethren, what shall we do? Then Peter said unto them, Repent, and be baptized every one of you in the name of Jesus Christ for the remission of sins, and ye shall receive the gift of the Holy Ghost. For the promise is unto . . . all that are afar off, even as many as the Lord our God shall call." "And they, continuing daily with one accord in the temple, and breaking bread from house to house, did eat their meat with gladness and singleness of heart, praising God, and having favour with all the people. And the Lord added to the church daily such as should be saved" (Acts 2:37-39, 46, 47).

7. The Holy Spirit Blends Conviction With the Possibility of Being Righteous. "And when he is come, he will reprove the world of sin, and of righteousness, and of judgment" (John 16:8).

Understanding the work of the Holy Spirit relieves us of the galling idea that we are to point out the bad habits of others to bring them to conviction. It also relieves us of the mistaken idea that we are to keep looking at our own unworthiness to be saved.

What a change would take place in homes and in churches were Christians to grasp the wonderful truth that the third person of the Godhead is the one who has the power and the authority to bring conviction. He brings reproof in such a beautifully balanced way, assuring the sinner of possible righteousness and of appearing in the judgment safe in Christ's righteousness.

The Holy Spirit does not bring galling reproof to us. He wants us to know that if we believe in and surrender to Christ, the judgment that was to fall on us will eventually fall on Satan. Thus not we but "the prince of this world is judged" (verse 11).

8. People Who Are Guided by the Holy Spirit Are Known by Their Fruits Rather Than by Gifts Such as Tongues (Matt. 7:16). "The fruit of the Spirit is love, joy, peace, longsuffering, gentleness, goodness, faith, meekness, temperance" (Gal. 5:22, 23).

Having a true Bible picture of the fruit of the Spirit, we do not fall into the error of equating the Holy Spirit with merely external living. We know what fruit should be in our lives when the Holy Spirit reigns supreme. If the fruit is not there, let us ask the third person of the Godhead to come into our own lives.

9. We Can Look to Him for the Gift of Love. "The fruit of the Spirit is love" (Gal. 5:22). "The love of God is shed abroad in our hearts by the Holy Ghost which is given unto us" (Rom. 5:5).

10. We Can Look to Him for the Gift of Joy. "The fruit of the Spirit is . . . joy" (Gal. 5:22).

11. We Can Look to Him for the Gift of Peace. "The fruit of the Spirit is . . . peace" (Gal. 5:22).

"But the Comforter, which is the Holy Ghost, whom the Father will send in my name, he shall teach you all things. . . . Peace I leave with you, my peace I give unto you: not as the world giveth, give I unto you. Let not your heart be troubled, neither let it be afraid" (John 14:26, 27).

12. To Receive the Holy Spirit and His Fruit, We Must Believe. "Now the God of hope fill you with all joy and peace in believing, that ye may abound in hope, through the power of the Holy Ghost" (Rom. 15:13).

13. The Holy Spirit Leads People to Obey by Creating a New Heart That Wants to Obey. "A new heart also will I give you, and a new spirit will I put within you: and I will take away the stony heart out of your flesh, and I will give you an heart of flesh. And I will put my spirit within you, and cause you to walk in my statutes" (Eze. 36:26, 27).

14. We Ask for the Holy Spirit Before Every Sermon, Bible Study, and Home Visit. "If ye then, being evil, know how to give good gifts unto your children: how much more shall your heavenly Father give the Holy Spirit to them that ask him?" (Luke 11:13).

A Personal Message

Many years ago the Holy Spirit used us as instruments in winning Maria to the Lord. Maria was in her midteens at the time. Her heart was deeply touched by the Spirit, and she requested baptism.

Years later, we were invited to conduct a series of meetings at a Christian college where Maria was enrolled as a student. Hardly had we arrived when Marie sought us out. She told us that she loved us as deeply as when she was baptized but that she was no longer a Christian.

As she shared the sad fact of her current spiritual status, our hearts were touched deeply. We loved Maria almost as if she were our own daughter.

We were impressed to tell Maria that she would regain her relation with the Lord Jesus during our week of meetings. But though Maria was kind and loving, she indicated that her decision was final. She would not consider being a Christian again. There was a tone of finality in her voice as she spoke.

But we sensed that Maria was not bitter toward God, just discouraged. She had not lived the life in Christ she had anticipated when she was baptized, and did not want to be a hypocrite. Recognizing that this was the situation, we assured her most kindly that we would claim the Spirit-laden promises for her renewal in Christ that week, and that she would really find a new power in her life.

Maria attended every meeting that week, but slipped out of the auditorium each time the call to surrender to the Lord was made. But the power of the Holy Spirit was so strongly felt that she decided she would not attend the last meeting, which was to be at eleven o'clock Sabbath morning.

When she thought that the meeting was closing, she made her way over to the auditorium to bid us good-bye. But to her surprise, we were still extending the call to accept Christ. Many were responding to make a new, or renewed, commitment to the Lord.

Maria found herself walking up the aisle, but when a Christian woman expressed delight because of this, she rushed back out of the auditorium to her dormitory room. After a time she returned, thinking that the meetings surely would be over by now. To her amazement—and ours—the response to our call was so great that people were still finding their way to the front.

Maria felt a power taking over that she could not withstand. She walked down the aisle hesitantly, as if trying to resist the power of the Holy Spirit. When she came as near the front as the crowded aisles would permit, she gave me a look as if to say, "You made me do this, but I did not want to."

I invited the audience to bow in prayer, and asked God to give repentance to everyone who had come forward. I was thinking primarily of Maria, who felt she was being forced to the front.

An hour or so after the meeting closed, Maria came to our room, her face beaming with delight. She told us she had been in the tortures of hell that week, but as I prayed for her repentance, she had experienced heaven in her heart.

Many Christians make the mistake of thinking that the backslidden soul has chosen to be lost, that he wants to go to hellfire. This is not true. Maria was sincere. But not having lived the life she felt she should, and not wanting to be a hypocrite, she had decided not to make a profession. God knew all the time that what she needed was the power of the Holy Spirit, which is promised in the Word of God (see Zech. 4:6; 10:1).

You may believingly ask and triumphantly claim the power of the Holy Spirit in your witness for the Lord. We do not need to use human pressure to try to shame a sinner into doing right. We need not belittle, scold, or take on a holier-than-thou attitude. The Holy Spirit can do more in a moment than we can do in a lifetime. So let us "ask of the Lord rain in the time of the latter rain" (Zech. 10:1).

Quiz

1. "Not by might, nor by power, but by my ...., saith the Lord of hosts" (Zech. 4:6).
2. A man must be born again of water and the .... (John 3:5).
3. "When he, the Spirit of truth, is come, he will .... you" (chap. 16:13).
4. Jesus said that the Holy Spirit "will testify of ...." (chap. 15:26).
5. We receive .... to witness to Christ after the Holy Ghost comes upon us (Acts 1:8).
6. The Holy Spirit restores to us the .... of salvation (Ps. 51:12, 13).
7. The Holy Spirit reproves of .... (John 16:8).

Correct Answers

1. spirit
2. Spirit
3. guide
4. me
5. power
6. joy
7. sin

Assignment

We claim the promise of the Holy Spirit in connection with sermons, counseling sessions, and personal visits. But we need Him on every occasion. So we strongly recommend that you claim the promise of His presence several times each day. You can do it in your heart at the very time you are conversing with another.

13

"STAKE YOUR CLAIM!"

Strengthening Your Faith "Muscle"

Some friends of ours secured mineral rights from the government on a particular parcel of land. In gaining the rights, they had to meet certain conditions in addition to staking and filing their claim.

Our Lord has promised us the gold of faith and love (Rev. 3:18), but we are to use the faith He has given us in asking, believing, and claiming these blessings. We can stake our claim to the gifts He has promised. To help faith to strengthen, we share with you seven ways the Holy Spirit helped us to find an increase of faith in every time of need.

1. I Remembered God's Past Answers to Prayer. "And thou shalt remember all the way which the Lord thy God led thee" (Deut. 8:2).

For years I had been impressed with the way God's professed people of old "forgot" Him (see Deut. 32:18; Ps. 106:12, 21). I concluded that since forgetfulness of God leads to a weak, backslidden faith, remembering will lead to increased faith and confidence. This is in harmony with the principle "We . . . beholding . . . are changed into the same image" (2 Cor. 3:18). If we look at failure, our hearts will be filled with fear, and our faith will weaken.

So I started a "remembering" process by making a chart on a piece of cardboard measuring about 18 by 24 inches. First I made columns to which I supplied headings such as "cars," "churches," "healings," and "studies." Below each heading I briefly described various answers to prayers. Thus I could easily read down any column and quickly recall the miraculous operations of the Lord in my life.

This idea developed gradually, through using the principle of remembering God's mercies.

As I reviewed past miracles from our God of love, I remembered the promise "What time I am afraid, I will trust in thee" (Ps. 56:3). "I will remember the works of the Lord: surely I will remember thy wonders of old. I will meditate also of all thy work, and talk of thy doings" (Ps. 77:11, 12). "Remember his marvellous works that he hath done; his wonders, and the judgments of his mouth" (Ps. 105:5). "He hath made his wonderful works to be remembered" (Ps. 111:4).

On one occasion when I was very sick, I determined to do some mental drilling on God's wonderful works to others, as well as to ourselves. As I thought of His Word that made the worlds (see Ps. 33:6, 9), I cried out to God, "Your word was powerful enough to speak the worlds into existence."

I reviewed God's dealing in various ages. I traced the record of His dealings through the Old Testament and New Testament. He opened the Red Sea and let His people go through on dry land. He caused the walls of Jericho to fall down without human effort. I thought of the works of our Lord Jesus. I visualized the leper coming to Him and being healed. I imagined the woman with the issue of blood, who was healed according to her faith. On and on I went. I found that this "remembering" gave me peace and strengthened my faith. I realized the fulfillment of the promise of Isaiah 26:3: "Thou wilt keep him in perfect peace, whose mind is stayed on thee: because he trusteth in thee." To stay our minds on our Lord is to increase our faith.

I observed that whenever I found my faith weakening, talking about what God had done for me strengthened it. Try it out, dear student. It works for anyone. It is a principle by which faith may be strengthened.

2. I Looked Away From Circumstances. At one time I seemed almost about to lose my mind. I could see nothing but failure ahead. There seemed no ray of light whatever. As I looked at the dismal future, God's Spirit flashed this text into my mind: "We look not at the things which are seen, but at the things which are not seen: for the things which are seen are temporal; but the things which are not seen are eternal" (2 Cor. 4:18).

I knew that God was speaking directly to my heart. As I now remember it, I had not read this scripture in a long time. God was saying to me, "Stop looking at the problems. You have already recognized them. Problem-centeredness will not solve problems, *but there is power in looking to Me.*" I had great difficulty in turning my mind from the problems. They were so close, so stupendous. But as I cried to God, He helped me to look toward Him.

"Look unto me, and be ye saved, all the ends of the earth: for I am God, and there is none else" (Isa. 45:22). "Remember the former things of old: for I am God, and there is none else; I am God, and there is none like me" (chap. 46:9).

3. I Learned to Talk Faith Even When I Seemed to Have None. I scanned the Holy Scriptures and was reminded that men of faith talked faith, and sang faith when all was dark. Joshua's men shouted victory against seemingly absolutely impregnable walls (see Joshua 6).

Gideon's band of 300 shouted faith in the presence of a great enemy army. Paul and Silas, held fast in prison, sang faith at midnight, and were immediately delivered (see Acts 16).

The two Hebrew spies who talked faith upon their return from Canaan realized the fulfillment of God's promise, but the ten spies who talked doubt perished (see Num. 14:28-32).

I learned that God honors those using "faith muscle" rather than "doubt muscle."

4. I Prayed Often Before an Open Bible. When George Müller prayed before an open Bible, it did something to his faith. It is said that he received $7 million as gifts without soliciting a penny. He cared for thousands of orphans, sent many missionaries overseas, and gave away thousands of pieces of literature. So I took the Bible in my hands and claimed its promises. The gesture was good for my faith (see Rom. 10:17).

5. I Placed My Finger on a Bible Promise. There was a man who promised in writing that he would repay another man a certain sum he owed him at a certain time. When the time arrived, he forgot to pay. His creditor went to him, unfolded his letter, and he showed the man that he had promised to pay. He placed his finger right on the promise. It gave him assurance in asking and expecting an answer. So I placed my fingers directly on God's promise that applied to my need.

"Faith cometh by hearing, and hearing by the word of God" (Rom. 10:17).

6. I Used Supporting Promises of God's Word. Let me clarify what I mean by "supporting" promises. As I identify them, they are Scripture statements that say God will keep His word. They say God cannot lie. They declare God will never break His word. They are, to me, in a different category from "specific" promises.

Specific promises, as I categorize them, are promises for specific things, such as wisdom (James 1:5), guidance (Ps. 25:9), healing (Jer. 33:6), the Holy Spirit (Luke 11:13).

When I claimed a specific promise, such as the one pledging wisdom, I told God why I believed He was giving the wisdom promised. It was because "God is not a man, that he should lie; neither the son of man, that he should repent [change his mind]: hath he said, and shall he not do it? or hath he spoken, and shall he not make it good?" (Num. 23:19). (See also Joshua 23:14; Ps. 89:34; Isa. 54:10; Matt. 24:35; 2 Cor. 1:20; Heb. 6:17, 18; 2 Peter 3:9.)

7. I Lifted My Hands to Jesus My Intercessor and Provider. For years I had studied the teaching of the Scriptures regarding "lifting up holy hands" (1 Tim. 2:8; Ps. 141:2). I had learned that when Aaron was consecrated by Moses, his hands, containing items offered to God, were waved before the Lord (see Lev. 8:6-27).

I read the psalmist's statement "Let . . . the lifting up of my hands [be] as the evening sacrifice" (Ps. 141:2).

I knew the evening sacrifice was a lamb (Num. 28:4), which was a type of Jesus, "the Lamb of God" (John 1:29). So, as I lifted up my hands, I believed that this was a symbolic way of saying to the Lord, "I have no merits in my life. I have no worthiness of my own. But there is Jesus, the Lamb of God, standing between Your justice and my guilt. I am coming through His name, in His merits." The Father in heaven throws open the whole treasure house of the universe to Jesus His Son, who has made our prayer His own.

I discovered that this gesture in prayer, though not often used, brings great assurance, especially in times of trouble. It destroys Satan's insinuation that because of our unworthiness we cannot expect answers to prayers.

A Personal Message

Experience has taught us that one of the finest methods of getting through to others is to tell how God has helped us and others that we know of. This builds faith.

This was Christ's way of spreading the good news. He commanded the healed demoniac, "Go home to thy friends, and tell them how great things the Lord hath done for thee, and hath had compassion on thee" (Mark 5:19).

This is one of the Lord's chosen ways of soul winning. This is objective learning. One learns so much easier by observing the Christian life of another than by having someone point a finger at him and preach at him.

For many years I have known that one of the best ways to answer questions is to tell a story of someone's experience. Jesus' ministry was made up of telling stories and helping people.

There is one caution, however. We must watch ourselves to be sure that we do not do too much talking. If we are so inclined, it is well to ask God to give us wisdom to "pipe down." One of the most common errors in deeply sincere individuals is that they talk *too* much. Too much talk about the best Friend in the world can hurt.

The wise man has instruction for this tendency. He advised, "Withdraw thy foot from thy neighbor's house;

lest he be weary of thee, and so hate thee" (Prov. 25:17).

If you do not know whether you are in this category, ask some friend to be perfectly frank in analyzing you and do not be offended if he does.

Quiz

1. We are to .... all the way God has led us (Deut. 8:2).
2. In spiritual matters we are not to look at things that are .... (2 Cor. 4:18).
3. Paul and Silas .... at midnight (Acts 16:25).
4. "Faith comes by hearing, and hearing by the word of God" (Rom. 10:............).
5. "God is not a man, that he should ...." (Num. 23:19).
6. We are to .... up holy hands in prayer (1 Tim. 2:8).

Correct Answers
1. remember
2. seen
3. sang
4. 17
5. lie
6. lift

Assignment

Make a list of blessings you have received in answer to prayer. If you have several classifications, place them under their several headings, as I did.

Mention one of these blessings to friends, but don't share the entire answer unless they ask you to tell about it. Simply attract their attention by briefly describing the blessing. Then go no further unless they ask.

For example, if God has blessed you in raising money to purchase a car, you may start observing, "God certainly worked a miracle for me so I could get money to buy the car I bought." If they do not ask further, you will not go further. This is one way we may guard against overtalking. And some people may feel you are trying to pressure them in some way by telling them your story, so they back off. But if they ask, tell the story of answered prayer.

Carefully study their faces to make sure they are not merely trying to tolerate you.

And remember! Do not tell too much at one time!

14

ETERNAL LIFE NOW?
When Do We Receive It?

Years ago I taught a course on the technique of soul winning. As the students began practicing the seven secrets that I shared, excellent results followed.

Then we began to learn the science of the Prayer of Reception. We learned to combine the science of soul-winning communication with the science of prayer. We learned not to center on John Doe's bad habits, but to help him fix his gaze on the solution—Jesus Christ. You cannot cure one bad habit by practicing another. Centering our attention on how bad evil is cannot produce good. Only good begets good. Let us share some of our discoveries with you.

1. Pardon and Cleansing Are Offered Freely. We accept complete pardon, and then share the promise of pardon. "The good Lord pardon every one that prepareth his heart to seek God" (2 Chron. 30:18, 19).

We accept complete cleansing from sin, and then point others to the cleansing Christ. "I will pardon all their iniquities" (Jer. 33:8). "Though your sins be as scarlet, they shall be as white as snow; though they be red like crimson, they shall be as wool" (Isa. 1:18).

The same power that forgives and cleanses gives deliverance from sin. "Behold, I will bring it health and cure, and I will cure them, and will reveal unto them the abundance of peace and truth. And . . . I will build them, as at the first. And I will cleanse them from all their iniquity . . . and I will pardon all their iniquities, whereby they have sinned, and whereby they have transgressed against me" (Jer. 33:6-8).

Recently we received an urgent telephone call to visit two backsliders whom we shall call John and Jane Gray. Jane was pitifully crippled. Her Christian physician stated that she had more than twenty poisons in her bloodstream. Her condition seemed hopeless. Her husband, John, had slipped away from the Lord, and had lost his assurance of salvation and eternal life. And he was under personal condemnation because of bad habits that had conquered him. He sat there in their home downcast and full of guilt.

I read Jeremiah 33:6-8 to them and suggested that Jane insert her own name in place of the pronouns. We reread the passage, placing her name in it repeatedly. It promised her health. It promised her cure. It promised her peace and truth. As we enthusiastically placed her name in the heart of the promises, Jane seemed to grasp that these were for her personally.

But John continued to look despondent. We turned to him and suggested that he immediately think no more on his sins. We were claiming cleansing for him as well as pardon. We were claiming health and cure, and a rebuilding of both their lives. The promises we had read were for him personally, as well as for Jane, we said. We enthusiastically called on them to leave all sins of any kind at the foot of the cross. We encouraged them to ask, believe, and claim complete forgiveness, cleansing, and healing.

We prayed for healing for Jane's sick body. We invited her to pray a prayer of faith. She cried pitifully for forgiveness, cleansing, and healing.

John prayed briefly but emotionally. He and Jane were now looking away from their problems to Christ, the Solution for every ill. As we left the home, we urged once again that they continue looking toward the Solution—Jesus Christ. If symptoms returned, they should assert their freedom in Him.

Their Christian physician attended one of our meetings the following week. Speaking of the change in John's and Jane's lives, he summed it up in one word: "Unbelievable!" Yet he did believe. He saw the proof. John also testified that from the hour we taught them how to make the promises of God personal, his vile habit departed. It had no more power over him.

Do we need to repeat the important lesson? Let us not fix our minds upon our problems. Instead, let us set our faces in the direction of the Solution—Jesus Christ. Let us not focus on the habits. Instead, talk about Christ, our personal Saviour. There is no power in mulling over sin and wrong habits. Rather, "Look unto me, and be ye saved" is God's command (Isa. 45:22). By "beholding" we are changed "by the Spirit of the Lord" (2 Cor. 3:18).

2. Eternal Life Assured. We receive it when we truly receive Christ as Lord of our lives. "And this is the promise that he hath promised us, even eternal life" (1 John 2:25).

I remember the first time I placed my finger on this wonderful promise. I asked. I believed. I thanked God that I had received eternal life. I inserted my own name. It read like this: "And this is the promise that he hath promised Glenn Coon, even eternal life." This promise brought me glorious assurance.

We share the assurance we receive. "These things have I written unto you that believe on the name of the Son of God; that ye may know that ye have eternal life" (1 John 5:13).

Two men from what we call "Drugland America" were led to read of our experience and our suggestions that others follow it. These young men accepted our suggestions and believed that God would honor His pledges. With their fingers on 1 John 2:25, they claimed eternal life by placing their names in the promise. They accepted the promise with tears. Shortly they began sharing with others.

3. This Assurance Brings Hope. "That we through patience and comfort of the scriptures might have hope" (Rom. 15:4).

A drunkard staggered into one of our meetings and, after sitting through most of the service, came up to the front. Probably he intended to ask for money. Immediately, a young minister who had been a heroin addict for ten years stepped to his side. As he quietly talked, hope sprang up into the drunkard's mind. Then the poor man sobbed out his repentance to God. And God forgave him.

4. All Need Hope. Hope saves us. "For we are saved by hope" (Rom. 8:24).

We share this hope with others. "That which we have seen and heard declare we unto you, that ye also may have fellowship with us: and truly our fellowship is with the Father, and with his Son Jesus Christ" (1 John 1:3).

A 19-year-old drug addict, in deep agony over his habit, asked his mother what he should do. As she was searching for an answer, he spoke again. "If I knew there was even a single ray of hope . . ." He never finished the sentence.

5. Our Lord Is That Hope. "For thou art my hope, O Lord God: thou art my trust from my youth" (Ps. 71:5).

6. The ABC's of Personal Salvation. Acknowledge that you are a sinner. "Only acknowledge thine iniquity" (Jer. 3:13). To make it easier for us to acknowledge ourselves as sinners, think of how God has put *all* in the same class as ourselves. He says, "For all have sinned, and come short of the glory of God" (Rom. 3:23). Acknowledge that you deserve death: "For the wages of sin is death" (chap. 6:23).

Believingly behold the Lord Jesus Christ. "Believe on the Lord Jesus Christ, and thou shalt be saved" (Acts 16:31). Note the three names of our Saviour in this text: Lord, Jesus, Christ.

To believe on the Saviour as *Lord* means we acknowledge we have bungled our lives and so accept Him as our Ruler and the Director of our steps. It means that we recognize our own plans and purposes have not had good results, so we want to take a Master who is infinite in wisdom, power, and love. Therefore, we ask Him to be our Lord, we choose His leadership, we crave His guidance, we completely surrender to His Lordship.

We cannot obey Him in our strength, but we can choose Him as our Lord. When we choose believingly, we open our hearts. "For it is God which worketh in you both to will and to do of his good pleasure" (Phil. 2:13).

To believe on *Jesus,* means we grasp the promise "Thou shalt call his name JESUS: for he shall save his people from their sins" (Matt. 1:21). Jesus is "the Lamb of God, which taketh away the sin of the world" (John 1:29). The death that we deserve, He took. "He hath made him to be sin for us, who knew no sin; that we might be made the righteousness of God in him" (2 Cor. 5:21).

To believe on Jesus, then, is to believe that He died in our place and satisfied the demands of the broken law, which was death.

To believe on Jesus is to believe that "the blood of Jesus Christ . . . cleanseth us from all sin" (1 John 1:7).

To believe in the Divine One as *Christ,* which means

Messiah, the Anointed One (Acts 10:38), is to accept Him as the One who the Old Testament prophesied was to come to be the Redeemer of mankind, to be my Redeemer. It is to accept Him to be my heavenly High Priest (Hebrews 9, 10), and my great Advocate (1 John 2:1).

So, as we come truly confessing our sins in simple, childlike faith, we are cleansed. But more than this, we have Christ in our hearts through His Holy Spirit, which is given without measure (John 3:34). The Holy Spirit that anointed Christ gives us power to "confess" Him before men.

7. Life Eternal Is in Christ. "In him was life" (John 1:4). "And this is the record, that God hath given to us eternal life, and this life is in his Son. He that hath the Son hath life" (1 John 5:11).

8. Jesus Is My Saviour. When people ask us whether we are saved, we prefer not to make the subject of our reply "I" but rather "Jesus." So our answer can be, "Jesus is my Saviour." This places "Jesus" as my "Saviour" at the first and the last and myself right in the middle.

If I choose (God forbid) not to have Jesus any longer, then "he that hath not the Son of God hath not life" (1 John 5:12).

9. The Purpose of This Study. "These things have I written unto you that believe on the name of the Son of God; that ye may know that ye have eternal life, and that ye may believe on the name of the Son of God" (1 John 5:13).

A Personal Message

From the previous lesson it will be seen that our Lord promises us personal pardon. When we receive that, we are to begin sharing it immediately with another as God's providence opens the way.

As we were preparing this lesson we met a young woman who had wandered very far from God. She was planning to divorce her husband and marry another man, who happened to be a leading officer in his church. He had asked her to marry him as soon as he got a divorce from his wife.

The Holy Spirit impressed us to use three specific laws of soul-winning communication with this young woman, whom we shall call Helena.

We talked *faith*—not merely faith in the promises of God, but faith in her future. God's Word declares, "This is the victory that overcometh the world, even our faith" (1 John 5:4). God wanted, and we wanted, Helena to overcome the world. But this could be done only by faith. So we were impressed by the Lord to express fabulous faith in Helena. Satan tempted us to believe we were overdoing it, but "whatsoever is not of faith is sin" (Rom. 14:23). Helena could scarcely comprehend that we would express such confidence that she would have victory in her life. To express simple, warm faith in a person without preaching is important. It is a fellowshiping kind of faith, not a preaching kind.

We talked *hope.* "We are saved by hope" (chap.

8:24). For Helena's marriage to be saved, we had to let the Holy Spirit speak hope through us to her. We told her we believed she was destined to bless hundreds of individuals who, like her, had doubted God's pardon, and who, like her, had felt they had sinned too grievously to be forgiven.

We talked *love.* "We love him, because he first loved us" (1 John 4:19).

These three laws of soul-winning communication are implied in 1 Corinthians 13:13: "And now abideth faith, hope, charity [love]." "Charity never faileth" (verse 8).

As Helena talked with us, she stated that she really loved this married man and that he was a wonderful man. We did not tell her she was merely experiencing infatuation. Why should we, when we have the wonderful instruments of faith, hope, and love?

Three days later we met Helena again. Her face was filled with sweet assurance in Christ. What had happened? "I never thought I could do it," she told us. "But do you know, I called my husband last night, and confessed and apologized to him." He was dumb with astonishment at the change in his wife.

The laws of faith, hope, and love are not for the use of ministers only. They are for everyone who will learn the science of soul-winning communication, and who will blend this science with the prayer of faith.

As the Holy Spirit used us, we were claiming several promises for Helena. We were *asking, believing,* and *claiming* the answers.

As we have seen, there are hundreds of promises in the Bible. They fit any problem you may have. Find and learn as many of them as you can. As in commitment and faith you trust in God and His promises, He will work for you as He has for us. God answers. He is no respecter of persons.

Quiz

1. We are invited to believe on the .... Jesus Christ to be saved (Acts 16:31).
2. To believe on the Lord is to do the .... of His Father which is in heaven (Matt. 7:21).
3. Part of believing on Jesus is to know that He will save us .... our sins (chap. 1:21).
4. Christ, a name meaning *anointed,* was anointed with the Holy Ghost (Acts 10:38). He promises us the same anointing through the .... (chap. 1:8).
5. "He that hath the Son hath ...." (1 John 5:12).

Correct Answers
1. Lord
2. will
3. from
4. Spirit
5. life